THE MESSIAH

JACQUES DUQUESNE

THE MESSIAH

An Illustrated Biography of Jesus Christ

Flammarion

Jesus declared publicly: Whoever believes in me believes not in me but in the one who sent me,
and whoever sees me, sees the one who sent me. I have come into the world as light,
to prevent anyone who believes in me from staying in the dark any more. If anyone hears my words
and does not keep them faithfully, it is not I who shall judge such a person, since I have come not to judge
the world, but to save the world

John 12 : 44–47.

PAOLO VERONESE, *SUPPER IN THE HOUSE OF SIMON*, 1570.
PINACOTECA DI BRERA, MILAN.

ONTENTS

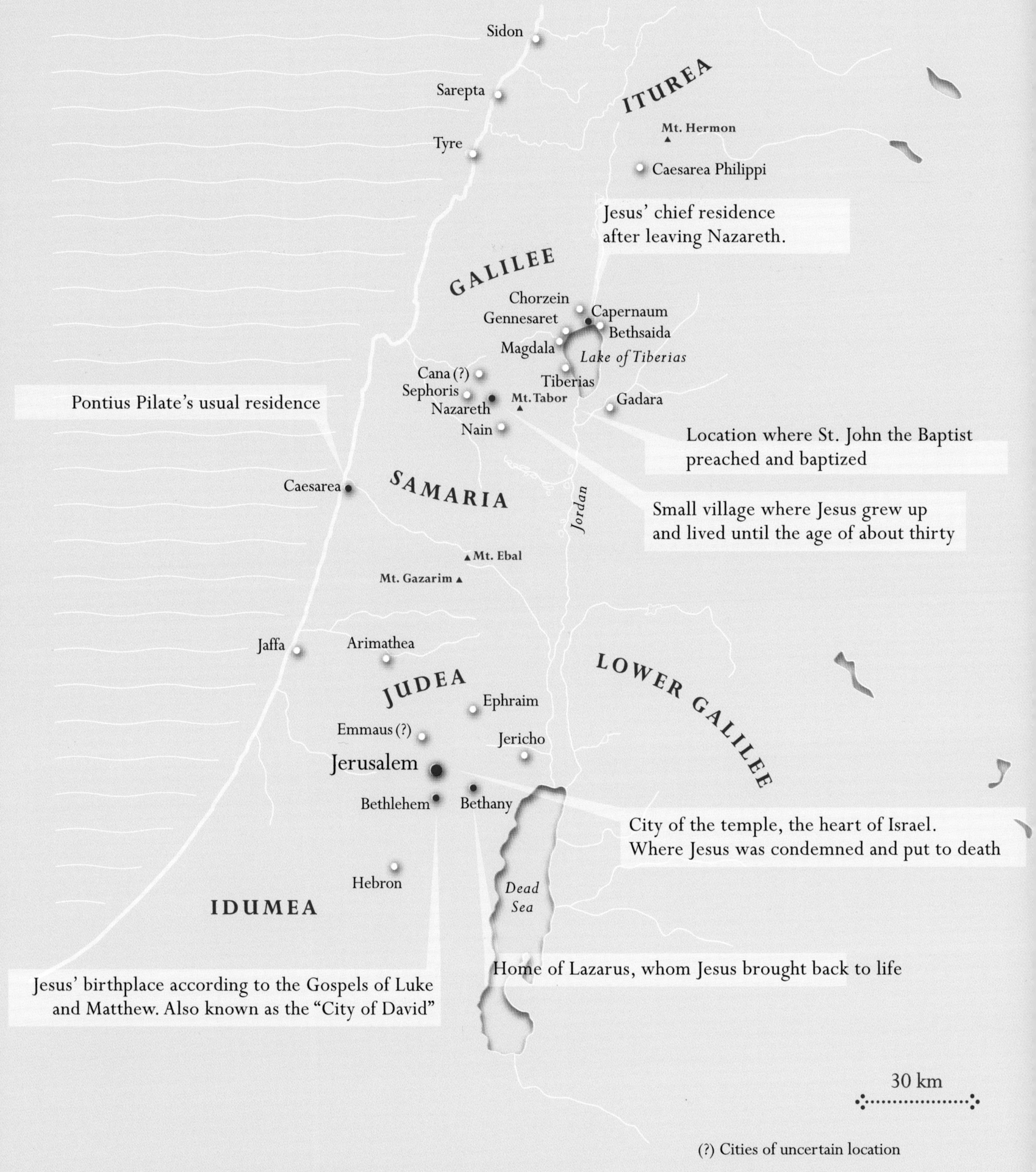

Sidon

ITUREA

Sarepta

Mt. Hermon

Tyre

Caesarea Philippi

Jesus' chief residence
after leaving Nazareth.

GALILEE

Chorzein
Capernaum
Gennesaret
Bethsaida
Magdala
Lake of Tiberias
Cana (?)
Tiberias
Sephoris
Nazareth   Mt. Tabor
Gadara
Nain

Pontius Pilate's usual residence

Location where St. John the Baptist
preached and baptized

Small village where Jesus grew up
and lived until the age of about thirty

Caesarea

SAMARIA

Jordan

Mt. Ebal

Mt. Gazarim

LOWER GALILEE

Jaffa

Arimathea

JUDEA

Ephraim

Emmaus (?)

Jericho

Jerusalem

Bethlehem   Bethany

City of the temple, the heart of Israel.
Where Jesus was condemned and put to death

Hebron

Dead
Sea

IDUMEA

Home of Lazarus, whom Jesus brought back to life

Jesus' birthplace according to the Gospels of Luke
and Matthew. Also known as the "City of David"

30 km

(?) Cities of uncertain location

JESUS, FULLY GOD, FULLY MAN

His name was *Yeshua*, a Hebrew first name, which means "Yahweh (Jehovah) saves." Even before he had departed this earth he was called Christ, from the Greek *Christos*, which signifies chosen of God, at one with God, in God—a term implying that, for his disciples and down through the centuries, he is both fully man and fully God at the same time.

This assertion is the most astonishing ever proffered by any religion and constitutes the absolute originality of Christianity. It has always been a struggle to get that belief accepted—and is still so today. According to the apostle Paul, both Jews and pagans found outrageous, even crazy, the idea that this Christ, "the power of God," would take on the human condition to the point of bitter torture and death. While in the second century the Greek philosopher Celsus affirmed that this belief in a God-Man was the "most shameful of all the Christians' claims." Whether or not one accepts the "claim" of the Incarnation, it is undeniable that this *Yeshua,* who becomes first *Iesous* in Greek and then "Jesus" in the West, transformed the history of the world.

Our planet's history is divided into "before" and "after" him. And while his divinity might be questioned, the message that he brought and bequeathed to us is unique. In his time as in ours, thirst for power vied with thirst for power, cruelty with cruelty, hatred with hatred. But he, and he alone, declared: "Love your enemies." Not just: "Love each other," which other Jewish preachers and rabbis were saying at the time. But love those who hurt you, who are in your way, who irritate you, who spread calumnies and lies about you, who insult you, who steal from you or wound you. This doesn't mean one has to let them have their way: but while combating them one has to love them. The toughest and most beautiful of all messages of love.

The story of the God-Man is so incredible that some went so far as to deny Jesus' very existence. But now, faced with the wealth of testimony, not a single serious historian would do so today. First, there is the account of a Jewish Roman citizen, with a Greek education, named Paul, who wrote about Jesus to the inhabitants of Thessaloniki some fifteen years after the Crucifixion. Then there are the four so-called "canonical" Gospels (the ones whose validity is vouchsafed by the Christian Church): that of Mark, which many scholars date to about 70 CE in Rome; that of Matthew, perhaps written initially in Aramaic (a language spoken throughout the Middle East and doubtless by Jesus and his companions), but which we know only by a final version, in Greek, probably dating from the 80s; that of the Greek author Luke, written at the same time; and that of John, who quotes Jesus' sayings more than the events of his life (except, notably, the Passion), which survives in a version dating from the end from of the first century—apparently the fourth derivation from an original text.

To the above can be added the Acts of the Apostles, which tell of the beginnings of Christianity and the Epistles, addressed to the fledgling Christian communities by some of the disciples. All of these writings have been argued about, pored over, and pulled apart, surely more than any other manuscripts of the period. Among them some significant differences concerning the description of the events, indications of time and place do exist: but today it is recognized that these stem mainly from diverse testimonies based on real happenings. In fact, if a group had wanted to found a religion artificially, they would have made their stories match. It should be added that the narrators seem very close to the history they relate, a very rare phenomenon in documents from Antiquity.

Other attestations of the existence of Jesus are non-Christian in origin. One might quote the Jewish historian Flavius Josephus, born in Jerusalem only seven years after Jesus' disappearance, who, in the 90s in Rome, composed *The Jewish Antiquities,* a history of his people during the century. In particular he mentions the stoning to death in 64, on the order of the high priest Annas, of James, a "brother of Jesus called Christ." He also informs us that Herod had put to death "a good man," John, "called the Baptist," who exhorted "the Jews to practice virtue, to act justly the ones to the others and piously towards God."

Three Latin authors writing at the very beginning of the second century also provide indirect testimony of Jesus. Pliny the Younger, Roman consul, governor in Asia Minor and a brilliant orator, in a letter to Emperor Trajan refers to inhabitants who refuse to adore the imperial image, singing together "an anthem to the Christ as well as to God." The historian Tacitus is more explicit. In reference to the conflagration that engulfed Rome in 64—a fire for which some were blaming Emperor Nero—he writes: "To stifle the rumor, Nero produced the culprits and subjected to the most refined torments a people much hated for their turpitudes, the people called 'Christians.' This name comes to them from Christ, who, during the rule of Tiberius, had been put to death under the procurator Pontius Pilate; suppressed at that time, this execrable superstition again raised its head not only in Judaea, the cradle of the evil, but even in Rome."

This was the time when little bands of the city's Christians, presented by Tacitus as the lowest of the low, were disposed of in Roman circuses for the entertainment of exhausted troops returning from the colonial battlefields. Another historian, Suetonius, confirms him on this point: "Christians, a kind of people devoted to a new and dangerous superstition, were tortured to death."

In addition, there exists a smattering of archeological discoveries in relation to the life of Jesus and the onset of Christianity. In 1961, in the Roman theater at Caesarea (where, finding it hard to secure a foothold in Jerusalem, the Romans had established their capital), a statue base was unearthed bearing the names of Tiberius and Pontius Pilate, presented as governor of Judaea. The discovery is all the more interesting since, up to that point, apart from in the Gospels, Pilate had appeared only in the writings of Tacitus and Flavius Josephus, as well as on a few coins. Another discovery, brought to light by chance during excavation work in Jerusalem in 1968, confirms sometimes contested details provided by the Evangelists regarding the Crucifixion. Workers found the skeleton of another man crucified in the first century, whose heels had been transpierced by a seven-inch long nail and whose legs were deeply bent. Though it is true that the Romans practiced crucifixion in various ways, the surviving relevant documents generally correspond to the texts of the Gospel.

Lastly, a pinpoint analysis of these texts has unearthed further clues to their authenticity. One example is the well-known parable of the Pharisee and the tax collector in which the former steps forward as he prays in the Temple, while the latter holds back, castigating himself. Jesus had the Pharisee say: "I thank you, God, that I am not grasping, unjust, adulterous like everyone else, and particularly that I am not like this tax collector here" (Luke 18:11). This is puzzling in that the formula "I thank you, God," occurs only once in all of the Old Testament, at the beginning of a poem by Isaiah. Neither is it to be found in Jewish texts from the first centuries of the common era. Where did Jesus come up with such an invocation? The puzzle was not solved until the twentieth century with the discovery of the famous manuscripts at Qumran. The phrase "I thank you, God" was employed fourteen times (out of eighteen) at the beginning of hymns sung by the Essenians, a Jewish splinter group, who almost all lived well outside cities and villages, and observed a strict ascetic way of life. Not only does this add weight to Luke's text, but it also shows that Jesus had a sense of humor, putting an Essenian expression into the mouth of a Pharisee, when the two groups were not on friendly terms.

Similarly much has been made of the meal taken by Jesus with a "publican" (customs or tax collector) named Levi (Mark 2:14–17). The Evangelist says that Jesus had found Levi "sitting at the tax office," which implies the existence of a border at that place, between Capernaum and Bethsaida. While for centuries no traces of it were unearthed, we now know that a border once existed, but it was removed after the year 39, under the rule of Agrippa I, when the eastern and western parts of Jordan were unified.

Specialists in Gospel exegesis also have developed criteria of authenticity allowing the historicity of other statements or actions to be verified. The criteria are of several types. First of all, they study the language used. Since Jesus spoke Aramaic, sentences in the Gospels containing words in that language (or phrases that can be readily back-translated into it) are probably authentic. Another criterion is "inconvenience." Whenever deeds or words assigned to Jesus seem in contradiction with the image, you might guess that they were genuine. A classic example is the anointing of Jesus by John the Baptist. It is hard to see why Jesus, free of sin, needed to be baptized. Moreover, for several decades, disciples of John the Baptist claimed he was superior to Christ. The Evangelists' reluctant mention of the baptism surely indicates that it was a fact they could not hope to conceal—and therefore that it truly happened. We pass over certain other criteria (and there are many), such as the multiple occurrences of a single phrase or a particular word that runs throughout the entire teaching of Jesus.

But one important factor is a lack of originality, which specialists, in their jargon, call "dissimilitude." The principle is simple: in the words recorded as being of Jesus, you should be suspicious of words and phrases also found in Judaic texts—that may have been simply copied. Another thing to watch for is a seamless conformity with concepts forged by the early Church, since they might have been slipped into the texts by over-zealous disciples. This said, such a criterion must be handled with caution since neither the Judaism of the time nor the ideas adopted by the earliest Christian communities are perfectly known. Moreover, Jesus did not break totally with Judaism and obviously his ideas underpinned those of the early Church. In this respect, one expression passes the originality test. Like the commandment "Love your enemies," it was first used by Jesus. This is the word "*abba*" which he employed to address God and can be translated more or less as: "Dearest father." Not only is it absent in Jewish liturgical prayers of the time, but it also expresses a degree of intimacy that is utterly unique and thus did much to strengthen faith in the divinity of Jesus. No one is obliged to believe in this divinity, of course. True love cannot be commanded. A God of love could not, and would not want to force belief on people. The revolution that Jesus incited was rooted in the revelation of a liberating God.

This book is based on texts of the New Testament—the history they tell, but also the symbols and teachings they offer. It is illustrated with the most beautiful, most meaningful depictions, through which over the centuries people have tried to express the coming of Jesus. It can be used as an aid to prayer, to thought, and, most especially, to question what humanity might be like today if we were to take up and make our own the simple three-word precept, "Love your enemy."

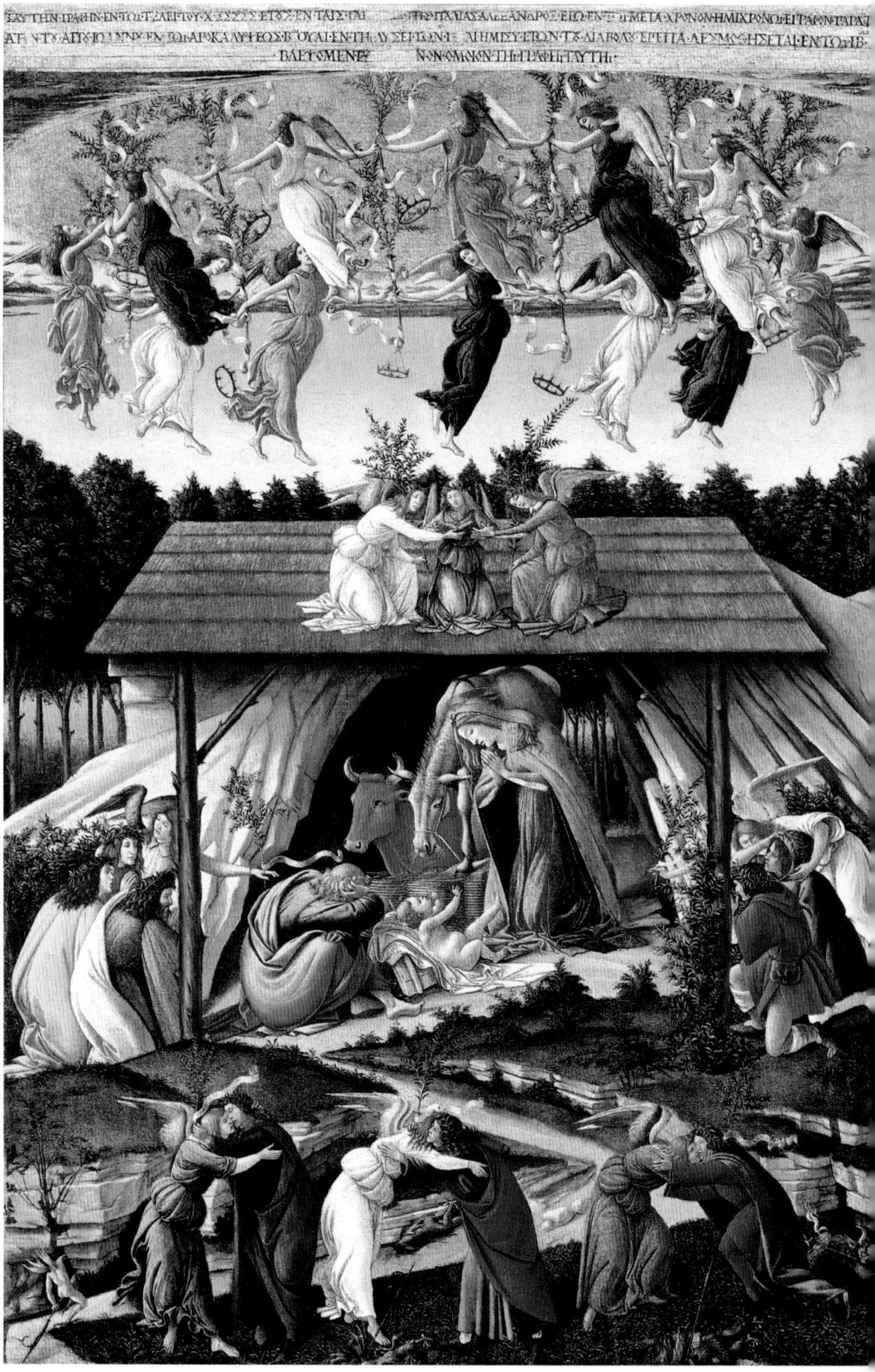

THE INCARNATION

But you (Bethlehem) Ephrathah,
the least of the clans of Judah,
from you will come for me
a future ruler of Israel whose
origins go back into the distant
past to the days of old. Hence
Yahweh will abandon them only
until she who is in labor gives
birth (Mic. 5:1–2).

"You see before you the Lord's servant. Let it happen to me as you have said"

(Luke 1:38).

THE ANNUNCIATION
AND THE VISITATION

•:··················:•

"Rejoice!" These were the first words of the Archangel Gabriel's Annunciation to Mary in the Gospel of Luke, the only one of the Evangelists to record the scene, which has been passed down in liturgy and spirituality and made famous through art and literature. "Rejoice!" The whole story is filled with joy. A girl, scarcely more than a child (betrothed to Joseph, so probably thirteen or fourteen), received an unbelievable message: she would give birth to a son who would ascend to the "throne of his ancestor David" and "his reign will have no end" (Luke 1:28–33). Mary might have guessed that he was the Messiah for whom the Jewish people were waiting. We are told that "she was deeply disturbed by these words" (Luke 1:29) and went to visit her cousin Elizabeth, herself pregnant with John the Baptist, who "leapt in her womb" (Luke 1:1). At once Elizabeth spoke to her of joy and happiness. Mary answered with a song, known as the "Magnificat" that begins, "My soul proclaims the greatness of the Lord and my spirit rejoices in God my Savior" (Luke 1:46–47). Her only wish was to believe and to rejoice.

True joy comes from sharing. And this is why, Luke continued, Mary did not hesitate to announce the good news to her cousin, though Elizabeth did not live next door and she had to travel into "hill country." Such a trip was no holiday, especially for a woman so young.

This account echoes the Exodus and its journey to another place—a frequent biblical theme. The first order God gave to Abraham was "Leave your country, your kindred and your father's house for a country which I shall show you" (Gen 12:11). In other words: turn your back on your past and go to the place indicated by God, towards the unknown. Abraham did not know what awaited him, nor where God wanted to lead him. Yet, he still went. And the youthful Mary also went, traveling through a mountainous and almost deserted area, less lush than the green and flowery Galilee, towards the future.

She might have thought that the child announced to her would be the Jewish Messiah, as she had been taught: a royal personage, a scion of the line of David, an instrument of God, who would save Israel from the enemy, from all its enemies.

LEONARDO DA VINCI. *THE ANNUNCIATION*, C. 1474.
GALLERIA DEGLI UFFIZI, FLORENCE.

"Rejoice you who enjoy God's favor. The Lord is with you"
(Luke 1:28).

"Of all women you are the most blessed and blessed is the fruit of your womb"
(Luke 1:42).

The book of Samuel tells us that God promised David he would be the head of Israel, and David became its king at the age of thirty. On his deathbed, he transmitted the office the Lord had entrusted to him to Solomon, his son: "If your sons are careful how they behave, and walk loyally before me with all their heart and soul, you will never wait for a man on the throne of Israel." (I Kings 2:4). But the "pastors of Israel" had been "bad shepherds," as the book of Ezekiel underlines, and the kings of Israel had been bad kings and the wait dragged on, punctuated by a series of ordeals. At the time Mary lived, the Jewish community was waiting for a Messiah who would restore the country's independence, with Jerusalem as its capital. No one expected him to be of divine origin. The words "Son of the Most High" (Luke 1:32) that the angel Gabriel used in reference to Mary's child did not necessarily mean he was divine. And they had been used before—in the Old Testament prophets were often called Sons of God.

Most theologians and exegetes concur that Mary was not immediately aware of the divinity of Jesus. Still, carrying the Messiah, and in such conditions, was something she had never asked, or even hoped, for. She was going to marry Joseph the carpenter, as their families had agreed, and she was already promised in marriage, almost his wife (at this time marriage occurred in two stages: a reciprocal betrothal, followed, after a delay of variable length, by the entry of the bride into her husband's house). Suddenly she was faced with a completely unforeseen situation. And yet, according to Luke, she had no hesitation: she trusted and had faith.

Yet she was also a bit of a realist, asking the angel: "But how can this come about, since I have no knowledge of man?" (Luke 1:34). She clearly understood the risks. The unborn child could well be the Messiah—she believed that he was—but in the meantime the gossiping tongues of Nazareth would have a field day. And what would Joseph think? She did not even ask Gabriel to go and inform her betrothed himself—a difficult job for her. According to Matthew (the only Gospel, in addition to Luke, which speaks of the birth of Jesus), Joseph already knew of the pregnancy and was planning to repudiate Mary in secret. But such a secret repudiation was impossible in the country at the time. Among other things, the presence of witnesses was required. Then an "angel of the Lord appeared to him in a dream and said 'Joseph son of David, do not be afraid to take Mary home as your wife, because she has conceived what is in her by the Holy Spirit'" (Matt. 1:20).

Luke's and Matthew's accounts provide a picture of the tricky situation in which the young couple found itself. Though their precise historicity is much discussed, and they are even somewhat contradictory, several lessons can be drawn from them. And it is surely these lessons that their authors sought to convey, more than exact and proven facts.

They present, at the outset, portraits of both Mary and Joseph. Mary is overjoyed, trusting in spite of the foreseeable risks, a realist but one committed to the future whatever it holds. Joseph is ready to forgive what he might think of as a mistake—a generous and trusting individual then. Saint John Chrysostom was even of the opinion that Joseph's act of faith and his acceptance was more laudable still than that of Mary, who had at least been forewarned by an apparition.

Second lesson: Jesus is the keystone that bridges Israel and Christianity. Not content to merely draw up genealogies for Jesus (be they contradictory or debatable) that link him back in particular to David, Jacob, and Abraham, the Evangelists Luke and Matthew wanted to show that he was only accomplishing what the prophets announced. Moreover, when Mary visited her cousin Elizabeth, already several months pregnant, the child (John the Baptist) "leapt in her womb" (Luke 1:41), a phrase Luke repeats as if to stress it. In the eyes of a number of specialists, this greeting embodies Israel's recognition of the great importance of the Jesus' coming.

The "Magnificat" by which Mary answers Elizabeth repeats almost word for word several extracts from the sacred Jewish texts. Father Daniélou, a great exegete who would become a cardinal, noted: "In the Gospel of Luke, the canticles of the first section seem to be of his own composition, or liturgical texts used by him." They are extracts from the Psalms and from the prayer of Anna, who, centuries before Elizabeth, had also been infertile. And for the women of the Bible to become a mother was nothing short of an obsession. After having long beseeched God, Anna finally gave birth to a son, the prophet Samuel.

Mary repeated Anna's prayer, but the language she used was stronger. The phrase from Anna's canticle "The bows of the mighty are broken, but the weak are girded with strength" (1 Sam 2:4) becomes in Mary's "Magnificat": "He has pulled down princes from their thrones and raised high the lowly" (Luke 1:52). And Luke then adds a whole new sentence: "He has filled the starving with good things, sent the rich away empty" (Luke 1:53). This text is significant: having learned that her son would be "Son of the Most High" and the successor of the great King David, Mary concluded—still according to Luke—that this was good news for the humble, the poor, and the hungry, and a curse on the rich and the replete.

According to Matthew, Jesus took up the same themes: "How blessed are the poor in spirit: the kingdom of Heaven is theirs" (Matt. 5:3). And "Blessed are those who hunger and thirst for uprightness: they shall have their fill" (Matt. 5:6). While the Gospel of Luke has: "But alas for you who are rich: you are having your consolation now" (Luke 6:24) and "Alas for you who have plenty to eat now; you shall go hungry" (Luke 6:25).

The accounts of the Annunciation and the Visitation thus constitute a kind of foreword. A foreword, which provides more than the bald historical facts: already it offers a meaning—the essential meaning.

And she gave birth to a son, her first son. She wrapped him in swaddling-clothes and laid him in a manger because there was no room for them in the living-space.

(Luke 2:7)

BIRTH

•:••••••••••••••:•

Bethlehem was a small, white village, a stone's-throw from Jerusalem. It was perhaps surrounded by wheat fields, since its name means "house of bread," but also by orchards since it was also called "rich in fruit." It was there that Luke and Matthew both place the birth of Jesus. Matthew stresses the fact that the prophet Micah (who, in the eighth century BCE, denounced the misdeeds of his compatriots) had announced that this large village would provide a leader "who would be shepherd of my people of Israel" (it is God speaking). Matthew was fond of showing how the life of Jesus paralleled what the prophets had predicted.

Yet he is not in total agreement with Luke on the circumstances of Jesus' birth. In the Gospel according to Matthew, everything seems to indicate that Joseph and Mary usually lived in Bethlehem. For Luke, on the other hand, they were already living in Nazareth, and had to travel to Bethlehem to take part in the census for "all the inhabited world" ordered by the Roman Emperor, Caesar Augustus. Each person had to be recorded in their own town, so with Mary "Joseph set out

from the town of Nazareth in Galilee for Judaea, to David's town called Bethlehem, since he was of David's House and line" (Luke 2:4).

A thorny question arises from this: no trace exists of this census (a complicated and prolonged operation at the time indicated by Luke). Some have wondered whether the authors of the "Gospels of Childhood" (the term given to the first few chapters of Luke and Matthew) have not located the birth-place of Jesus at Bethlehem simply to underline his descent from David. This is all the more possible since another Gospel, that of John, through various allusions, seems to regard Jesus as a native of Nazareth.

While it's not possible to be certain on this point, the significance lies elsewhere, in the fact that this birth itself passes completely unnoticed. Matthew does not even tell the story, though he goes on about the Holy Family's flight into Egypt (recalling Moses and the Exodus). As for Luke, he writes that the couple, since they had found no place in the city's over-flowing inns, sought refuge in a stable. And that Mary "gave birth to a son, her first-born. She wrapped him in swaddling clothes and laid him in a manger" (Luke 2:7).

You can hardly imagine a more sober description of such an event: there are no allusions to the marvelous here, rather a feeling of loneliness. On other occasions, the bible does not shy away from describing the birth process: cutting the umbilical cord, rubbing the belly of the child with salt before it is bathed, and finally swaddling it to prevent it moving its limbs, a precaution, it was thought at the time, that would make the baby stronger. The Gospels hardly touches on such details. The child is born, that's the important thing. In darkness and poverty: "No festooned drapes to preserve the child from the cold, only cobwebs hanging from the roof-beams," as Théophile Gautier put it, so typical of the many poets and writers of canticles and popular songs, keen to underline the unmitigated poverty of Jesus' birth.

The fact that the birth date too is unknown should not be surprising: no individual in Antiquity would have been able to give his date of birth, a detail which at the time was not recorded anywhere—except in the case of rulers to be. Looking at the Gospel of Luke, where shepherds sleep under the stars, it is unlikely that Jesus was born in December, since the weather, even in that climate, would have been cold for sleeping outdoors. A fourth-century Roman calendar reveals that it was only around the year 330 that people started celebrating Christmas on December 25. This date corresponds to the old Roman festival of the Sol Invictus, celebrated just as the sun seemed to be gaining in strength, when daylight began to encroach on the night. Jesus was sometimes actually represented as the sun: the oldest Christian mosaic in Rome, discovered in the twentieth

century beneath Saint Peter's Basilica, shows him borne in triumph on a chariot.

The celebration of Christmas was rapidly accompanied by customs, which, if they were symbolic at the start, soon became folksy. Advent candles standing for Christ's coming to bring light to mankind, have been transformed into multicolored electric garlands. The fir tree, which initially appeared in the Rhineland around the sixteenth century to represent the tree of Paradise, has become our Christmas tree. And the medieval origins of the crib are a subject of debate. As for the ass and the ox, they already appeared in the sixth century in an apocryphal Gospel (a term which means "secret," not recognized by the Christian Church) that refers to ancient prophecies with little obvious connection to the birth of Jesus. Henceforth, the ass and the ox were to appear at every crib and on many pictures accompanying the shepherds and the famous Magi or Three Kings.

Luke is relatively effusive on the shepherds. At the time, with their reputation for trickery and theft, they would have been treated as misfits. There was even a saying that went "do not rescue the *goïm* (heathens) and shepherds who fall down a well." Luke here underlines how Jesus had come for the excluded, for the poor—the same message he had stressed by transforming the words of the Psalms into Mary's "Magnificat." So according to Luke, Jesus' earliest companions were scarcely genteel. But the shepherds did not turn up by chance; they were chosen by an angel who sought them out. And while so many others hesitated to recognize Jesus, the shepherds went straight to the Child, quitting their herds, in spite of marauding bears, leopards, and jackals, as well as the robbers who infested the region. It is true—Luke could

So they hurried away and found Mary and Joseph, and the baby lying in the manger.
(Luke 2:16)

And going into the house they saw the child with his mother Mary,
and falling to their knees they did him homage.

(Matt. 2:11)

hardly avoid pointing out Jesus' divinity by adding "And all at once with the angel there was a great throng of the hosts of heaven" (Luke 2:13).

The Magi arrived later. According to Matthew, it was after their passage that King Herod—fearing in Jesus a future rival—ordered the massacre of all the region's children under the age of two. Since Herod died in 4 BCE, most specialists conclude that Jesus was born shortly before, between 4 and 6 BCE. The dating of "year 1" came from a miscalculation on the part of a sixth-century monk named Dionysius Exiguus.

The Magi, who were not kings at all, but astronomers and interpreters of dreams and exceptional events, came from the mysterious Orient. Matthew says that they were guided to Jerusalem by a star, which vanished when they reached the city. Unthinkingly, they decided to visit Herod in order to discover where "the king of the Jews" might be born. After consulting with his high priests, Herod pointed them in the direction of Bethlehem, where they found not a newborn baby, but a little child (*paidion* is the Greek word in the Gospel). They were then informed "in a dream" not to return via Jerusalem. This was prudent since reasons to be wary of Herod were known well beyond the confines of Judea. Herod, however, as is well known, had already taken things into his own hands and ordered the Massacre of the Innocents.

Within a few centuries, the Magi were endowed with identities. The one who, according to Matthew, brought Jesus gold as a mark of royalty, was named Melchior. Gaspar arrived with incense that was burnt in the presence of the gods. And finally, Balthazar, usually pictured with dark skin, presented myrrh, a balsam used to anoint the dead—a pre-figuration, it has been said, of Christ's entombment. Incense marked divinity and myrrh mortality—the dogma of the Incarnation, the faith in Jesus as God-Man, was thus symbolized. Lovers of folklore will be interested to learn that the famous *galette des Rois* (a crown cake in which a bean or a favor is hidden) was initially a French custom that appeared in the fourteenth century. Wealthy families would invite students and poor clerks for a meal on Twelfth Night. The person finding the bean would be awarded a sort of scholarship.

Known far and wide, accounts of Jesus' birth are thus laden with symbolism. The shepherds were destitute and scorned. The three kings were foreigners, present in order to show that Jesus came for all people. He arrived at night, into a world of darkness and doubt, in a minor city with little more than memories of a glorious past: the powerful Jews lived in Jerusalem, while the mighty Romans had set up their headquarters in Caesarea. From the beginning the powerful took fright and were prepared to do anything, including slaughtering the newly born, to exterminate Jesus, to stifle this voice before it could be heard and broadcast its message.

That is the meaning of the Gospels concerning Christ's birth.

ODILON REDON. *FLIGHT INTO EGYPT.*
C. 1903. MUSÉE D'ORSAY, PARIS.

CHILDHOOD

•:·················:•

No Old Testament text mentions Nazareth; nor do rabbinical writings of the time. It was a tiny village, with low and uncomfortable mud-brick houses surmounted by terraced roofs made of branches whipped together, laid on rafters and covered over with clay. Terraces could be reached by ladders or external stairways and the inhabitants would sleep there on hot nights, take meals there, and use them to dry laundry or fruit. The narrow passageways between the houses teemed continuously with gangs of boisterous children. The common picture of a well-behaved young Jesus living alone with Mary and Joseph is patently unlikely. Galilee was full of children (siblings, cousins, or close neighbors) running from house to house.

In Nazareth, as in the majority of villages, the peasants were smallholders, producing mostly olives, which were famous and exported all around the Mediterranean, wherever there were Jewish colonies. Olive cultivation demands great care and patience. The tree only reaches full yield after about fifteen years. A saying in Judea has it, not without a hint of envy, that it is "easier to grow olive trees by the myriad in Galilee than a child in the land of Israel." Curiously, in his parables, Jesus never speaks of the olive tree, though there is a "Mount of Olives" in Jerusalem.

Vines were cultivated everywhere, in particular in the South, in Judea. On the other hand, the fig grew in abundance in Samaria and in Galilee. Plutarch even wrote—with some exaggeration—that fruit from Palestine arrived in Rome every day for the emperor's table.

The peasants of Nazareth, even when landowners, also worked as paid laborers on larger domains, together with a handful of slaves. They would occasionally have experienced unemployment, as testified by the famous parable known as the "helpers of the eleventh hour," as reported by Matthew. Jesus tells of a great landowner looking for workmen for his vines. These he finds easily, "standing idle in the marketplace" (Matt. 20:3), at the third, sixth, even the ninth hour. Finally at the eleventh hour, as night is drawing in and he needs to finish urgently, perhaps because a storm is brewing, he goes back to

This was to fulfill what the Lord had spoken through the prophet:"I called my son out of Egypt"
(Matt. 2:15 [Hosea 11:1]).

ORAZIO GENTILESCHI,
*THE HOLY FAMILY AT REST
ON THE FLIGHT INTO EGYPT*, 1628.
MUSÉE DU LOUVRE, PARIS.

ANONYMOUS, *THE CIRCUMCISION OF JESUS*, C. 1347.
BASILICA SANTA MARIA MAGGIORE, BERGAMO.

the square and finds others still waiting. Asking a question that displays a supreme lack of awareness of the realities of their lives, he demands why they have stayed there all day long not working, to which the workmen answer simply: "Because no one has hired us" (Matt. 20:7).

The majority of these workers could hardly have eked out a living by the time they had paid their taxes to the Romans, the tithe (a tenth of the harvests) to the priests, as well as other charges. Though a fertile land, social inequalities in Galilee were beginning to aggrieve the inhabitants. From the time of Amos (who had started as a herdsman in the eighth century BCE), the prophets of Israel had unstintingly lambasted monopolies on land and capital, and had exaggerated consumption, injustice, and the obliviousness of the rich. And it was, of course, based on the realities he had known in his youth that Jesus described, in many parables, great estates with absent owners, managed by overseers who were often hard on the indebted peasantry.

Unlike Judea, Galilee was a center of immigration. Its name means "land of the Gentiles," or non-Jews. Phoenicians, Syrians, and Arabs settled there to cultivate the land and to trade, but also to rebuild Sephoris, Herod Antipas' capital,

destroyed during a revolt in 4 BCE. Herod was responsible for significant building projects in an imposing Greek style that resulted in an influx of migrant workers. It could be surmised that Joseph the carpenter and his son Jesus worked on Sephoris, though there is nothing to confirm this. The Gospels do not even mention the capital of Herod Antipas, who in about the year 26, decided to settle elsewhere.

What is sure, on the other hand, is that the Jews of Galilee, surrounded by so many pagans, were having an "identity crisis" and kept doggedly to their faith and rites. Recent archeological research seems to indicate that Nazareth was a hotbed of the Jewish religion and not a single vestige of a pagan symbol has yet been uncovered.

Specialists are convinced that Jesus must have received an extremely thorough religious education. From a reading of the four Gospels, it can be deduced that at a certain point in his childhood, or at the beginning of his adult life, he learned how to read and began commenting on the Hebrew Scriptures. He had at least some knowledge of biblical Hebrew, even if, like his compatriots, he spoke Aramaic.

A further sign of his family's profound faith comes from the annual pilgrimage made by Joseph and Mary to the Temple at

Simeon blessed them and said to Mary his mother:
"Look, he is destined for the fall and for the rise
of many in Israel, destined to be a sign that is
opposed—and a sword will pierce your soul too—so
that the secret thoughts of many may be laid bare"

(Luke 2:34–35).

GIOVANNI BELLINI, *"NUNC DIMITIS"*
(PRESENTATION AT THE TEMPLE), 1505–10,
THYSSEN-BORNEMISZA COLLECTION, MADRID.

RAPHAEL, *THE HOLY FAMILY WITH THE SACRED LAMB*, 1507,
MADRID, MUSEO NACIONAL DEL PRADO.

Jerusalem (according to the Gospel of Luke). Rebuilt by Herod the Great, for the Jews this Temple represented the heartbeat of the religious world. It was the home of the Holy of Holies. In this empty place the one God was both mysteriously present and absent (since God knows no bounds). It was a place where only the high priest could enter on the day of Yom Kippur, the Day of Atonement. Having kept apart, fasted, and purified himself, he would utter with awe the name of Yahweh and beseech Him to forgive the iniquities and offences of which His people, though chosen above all others, were guilty. And at the very moment that the high priest entered the Holy of Holies, the priests (approximately seven thousand, of which one thousand five hundred abided permanently in Jerusalem) and all the people knelt and prostrated themselves, asking that the Lord be forever praised.

The fact that Joseph and Mary traveled to Jerusalem each year shows that they were very pious. The annual pilgrimage to the Temple was only mandatory for men, and even they did not invariably comply with the rule, because the journey from Nazareth—some hundred and twenty kilometers away—was exhausting and often perilous. The route was a poor one, since those indefatigable road builders, the Romans, rarely made an appearance, leaving the country to their devoted henchmen, Herod and his sons. On approaching the capital, travelers had to cross a rocky and hilly stretch of land, peppered with caves, which were used as dens by bandits. Moreover, once there, the inhabitants of Jerusalem looked down on Galileans, making fun of their countrified accent, their stilted pronunciation, and reputation for obtuseness.

You can then only imagine the surprise of the doctors who, blithely initiating children in points of the Law, came upon the young Jesus. According to Luke his parents had taken him along "when he was twelve years old" (Luke 2:42) and, unable to see him among the caravan of Galileans returning home at the end of the pilgrimage, sought him high and low, finding him "in the Temple, sitting among the teachers, listening to them, and asking them questions, and all those who heard him were astounded at his intelligence and replies" (Luke 2:46–47). Many specialists doubt the historical basis of this story. It is found only in the Gospel of Luke, moreover in the highly contested first section. Perhaps it is a later interpolation, as its singularly pure Greek style would lead us to believe. No doubts need to be cast on the probability of the pilgrimage, however, as it was quite usual for pious parents to

And Jesus increased in wisdom, in stature, and in favor with God and with people
(Luke 2:52).

bring their son to the Temple, at least as he approached the age thirteen, later the age of the Bar-Mitzvah. Nor is it surprising that Jesus appeared better informed and more pious than the other children, as subsequent events were to confirm.

The doctors of the Law must have been all the more amazed since the boy was a Galilean, belonging in all probability to the "Am-Ha-Arez," meaning in theory, "people of the land," though the term was actually more pejorative and signified "hick" or "bumpkin." They were a people suspected of being lax with respect to the rules of the Law, and Rabbi Hillel, a wise man whose authority was held in great respect in the time of Jesus, even claimed that "an Am-Ha-Arez is incapable of piety."

As for the doctors of the Law, they were Sadducees, a people who controlled the Temple. They belonged to both a lay and a clerical (high priests, major priestly families) aristocracy who had to exercise honorable professions (lowly weavers and tanners, for example, were suspected of immorality). As an adult, Jesus would enter into conflict with this priestly caste. When the Gospels describe his debates with the scribes and the heads of the synagogue, even the Pharisees, the atmosphere seems relatively calm, even friendly. With the Sadducees, however, exchanges were far more abrasive. They played a crucial role in his death sentence.

As a child when Jesus walked out of the Temple to return to Nazareth, he could at last wear the prayer shawl, the *tallit*, and enter the synagogue; he could pronounce the blessings and hold up the scrolls of the Law for the faithful to worship. In religious terms, he had become of age.

The Two Herods

In general, Roman colonists relied on local leaders. This was the case with Herod, called "the Great," who with Roman approval, became King of Judea through a violent coup in 37 BCE. Many of his compatriots regarded him as only half Jewish (according to the historian Flavius Josephus, who was not very fond of Herod, his family had converted to Judaism only about fifty years earlier). Moreover, once recognized by the Romans, he had gone to the Capitol in Rome to offer a sacrifice to Jupiter in gratitude.

Sex, money, blood: these, if the accounts of the time are to be believed, were his principle interests. He exterminated the entire family of one of his wives, then had the woman herself murdered for good measure. Under the cover of night, he even snuck into David's tomb in Jerusalem to steal treasures. The list of his crimes goes on.

Nevertheless, Herod had a fine nose for politics. He extended the kingdom and almost succeeded in pacifying the country. Following a number of catastrophes—including famines and epidemics—he lowered taxes and even sold some of his own property to alleviate the suffering. He launched major reconstruction programs, the most significant being that of the Temple of Jerusalem, that "second Temple" the Jewish people had been dreaming about since the destruction of the first —that of Solomon. Herod was steeped in Greek culture and had built a dozen or so palaces in the Corinthian style, so the Jewish priests watched warily as he started their Temple. Yet he had some fine architects at his disposal, and, if outwardly Greek, the Temple respected all the demands of the Jewish Law.

Fittingly, Herod's life ended in blood and madness. Suffering, it is said, from ulcers and gangrene, he saw himself surrounded by enemies that he had to eliminate—starting three years before his death by two of his own children. He had planned for one of his offspring, Archelaos, to succeed him. But the Romans took a dim view of this choice and, following a civil war, had him exiled to Gaul. The kingdom was split between two of Herod's other heirs, Philip and Herod Antipas. The latter became tetrarch (viceroy) of Galilee and his reign was relatively prosperous and peaceful. According to Luke, Jesus called him "the fox." He imposed onerous taxes and was as crafty as his father. It was to him that Pilate sent Jesus following his arrest.

ANDREA SCHIAVONE, *CHRIST BEFORE HEROD*, C. 1550.
MUSEO DI CAPODIMONTE, NAPLES.

A Hidden Life

The "canonical" Gospels (those recognized by the Church) offer no information on Jesus' life between his pilgrimage to the Temple at the age of twelve and the beginning of his public proselytizing when he was about thirty. Even the apocryphal books, in spite of a wealth of more or less marvelous detail, say little more. Over the centuries, people wondered what Jesus could have been doing during this period, to the point that it has been termed the "hidden life."

Some have proposed that he adopted a monastic existence with the Essenians, a religious sect made famous by the discovery of the Dead Sea Scrolls in 1947. The Essenians followed an ascetic life, respecting with unbending rigor the demands of purity laid down by Scripture. Yet they were not above regarding themselves as the sole elect among the chosen people, something that runs counter to the all-embracing message of Jesus, who in fact neither preached nor adopted an ascetic or monastic life.

This thesis has thus been abandoned. Others have suggested that he trained as a priest, but there too there is no evidence. The term "rabbi" employed by his disciples merely means "master." Jesus thus remained a member of the laity. But he could read and write and was able to comment on complicated texts, with the implication being that he had spent the intervening years following advanced studies. At the same time, he would have surely continued to exercise his trade as a carpenter, all the while taking an interest in the agricultural world around him and perhaps even working in the fields, since his remarks as reported in the Gospels are peppered with allusions to farming.

A heated debate continues as to whether Jesus had brothers or sisters. If so, that would mean that he experienced life in a large family. There are references to just such a household and the brothers' names are even given, with at least twelve occurrences in the New Testament. The Roman Catholic Church, in affirming the perpetual virginity of Mary, proposes that they were probably cousins, but no longer condemns the increasing number of exegetes who translate the Greek adelphos, as employed in the Gospels, by the usual equivalent of "brother." Orthodox Churches often say that these were half-brothers from an earlier marriage on the part of Joseph, while today many Protestant congregations accept the existence of brothers and sisters.

Joseph

The Gospels, which already say very little about Mary (more verses are devoted to her in the Qur'an), have even less to say regarding Joseph. Matthew insists on a genealogy that makes him a descendant of David. In the same text he gives Mary's husband the most significant role. As mentioned earlier, an angel of the Lord appeared to Joseph in a dream, explaining that Mary had been made pregnant by the Holy Spirit. In a later dream the angel counseled him to take Mary and the Child to Egypt to flee Herod (Matt. 2:13).

Joseph named the child "Jesus," a highly significant act and a demonstration of authority at the time. It is thus through his father that Jesus was introduced to the social world and through him that he would learn a trade, and be brought to the synagogue (women were allowed only in a separate gallery), and receive religion lessons. The point is worth stressing: the father "fathered" his child through the relationship that bound him with his son, by the education that he gave him. As a carpenter, Joseph would have been a figure in the village. And for his community manual work was sacred. "A craftsman at his workbench does not need to stand up before the greatest doctor," went a rabbinical saying of the time. And carpenters, even poor ones, enjoyed particular consideration. The Talmud recounts that during a delicate debate in a lawsuit, it was sometimes asked: "Is there not among you a carpenter, or a son of a carpenter, who might answer the question?" The point was that in construction work the trade called for adherence to precise rules and the taking of exact measurements.

Unlike Mary, and those that the Gospels on several occasions term the brothers and the sisters of Jesus, Joseph was not mentioned in the texts by the time his son began to preach. His age at the birth of Jesus is unknown (the apocryphal books of the second century, determined to underline Mary's virginity, depict him as an old man). Christ became a public figure between the age of thirty and thirty-five, and it is most likely that Joseph had died in the meantime.

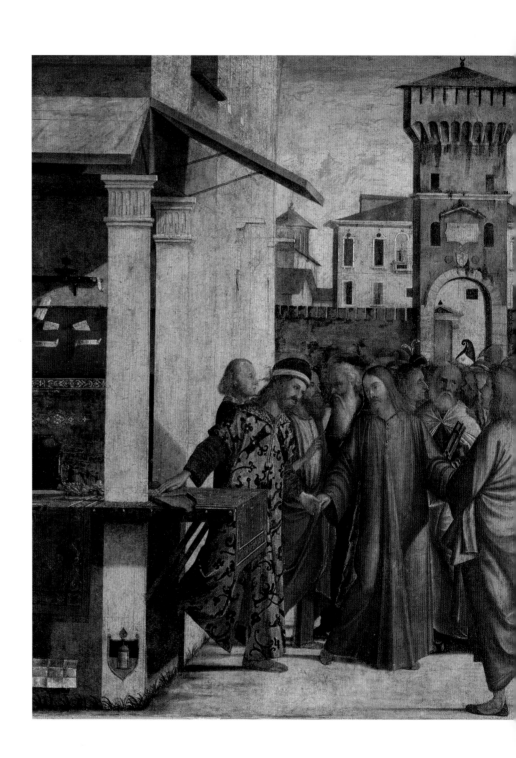

PUBLIC LIFE
BEGINS

A voice cries, 'Prepare in the desert a way for Yahweh. Make a straight highway for our God across the wastelands. Let every valley be filled in, every mountain and hill be leveled, every cliff be made a plateau, every escarpment a plain; then the glory of Yahweh will be revealed and all humanity will see it together, for the mouth of Yahweh has spoken'" (Is. 40:3 – 5).

*It was at this time that Jesus came from Nazareth in Galilee
and was baptized in the Jordan by John*
(Mark 1:9).

BAPTISM

•⋮⋯⋯⋯⋯⋯⋯⋮•

The Jordan is a capricious river that winds through the hills and plains to join Lake Genesareth (the Lake of Tiberias), at the Dead Sea. Sometimes it is a swirling torrent that brings down mud and branches. It is there that John (or Yohanon) preached. His was an extremely common first name: there were few given names at the time, so that the name of the father was always added to it, Zacharias (meaning "Yahweh has blessed him") in the case of John.

At the beginning of the first century, in about year 30, itinerant preachers were traveling from city to city and village to village announcing to the Jewish people that the time was nigh when God would come to their aid. Telling of the "apocalypse" (the word "apocalypse" did not have the negative meaning it has today, but signified "revelation"), they reassured an anxious people, fearful of straying from the Jewish Law and from God. For do not the high priests offer a bad example? They questioned why Herod and his sons had built Greek gymnasiums and theaters. They criticized the plays being staged at the theater in Jerusalem with roles for the

pagan gods. Such preachers, self-proclaimed prophets or eccentrics, comforted a nervous flock. They promised that better days were coming.

Yet John's harangues were very different. This ascetic, disheveled hermit berated his listeners, invoking the coming wrath of the Lord. As he explained, according to Matthew, being Jewish conferred no particular privilege: "Do not presume to tell yourselves, 'We have Abraham as our father,' because, I tell you, God can raise children for Abraham from these stones" (Matt. 3:9).

Such threats, however, did not deter the crowds—on the contrary. The historian Flavius Josephius even offered a lengthy description of this "good man exhorting the Jews to cultivate virtue and to employ justice in their relations amongst them and piety towards God." These injunctions to do good enjoyed such success that, according to John the Evangelist, the priests of Jerusalem dispatched a sort of board of inquiry to see what this troubling prophet was up to: What did he want? Who was he? His answer was, "I am, as Isaiah

And when Jesus had been baptized he at once came up from the water, and suddenly the heavens opened
and he saw the Spirit of God descending like a dove and coming down on him.
And suddenly there was a voice from heaven. "This is my Son, the beloved, my favor rests on him"
(Matt. 3:16–17).

prophesied: A voice of one that cries in the desert: Prepare a way for the Lord. Make his paths straight!" (John 1:23).

He thus made it clear that he was but a precursor. And he baptized, employing a new kind of baptism. As with all who lived in the desert or who had to cross it, the Jewish people ascribed a great many virtues to water. They multiplied purification rites using it; indeed at the time of Jesus and John, the Pharisees did so to the point of obsession. There were various forms of baptism at the time, but they had to be regularly repeated. John's method expressed the recipient's repentance and his espousal of a new life, in a foretaste of the forgiveness of sins on the day of the Last Judgment. More importantly, it was unique and final, even if John evoked that someone was coming after him "the one who is to baptize with the Holy Spirit" (John 1:33). This form of baptism constituted a singular challenge to the Temple and its priests, since through it one could obtain forgiveness of sins without the priests and their sacrificial rites.

John thus blazed a new path. Most crucially he announced Jesus. "I baptize with water; but standing among you—

unknown to you—is the one who is coming after me; and I am not fit to undo the strap of his sandal" (John 1:26–7). With rare agreement, except for one or two words, all four Evangelists use the same expression. But who exactly would have untied someone's sandals? When the tired master returned home one of his servants or slaves got down at his feet to do it. John thus considered Jesus as being so important that he would not be worthy of acting even as his servant. He knew that Jesus was coming soon, but said "I did not know him myself" (John 1:33). In other words, he did not really know him.

Perhaps John the Evangelist allotted these words to John the Baptist a posteriori because Jesus' and John's teachings would soon diverge. Their manner of living would too. John the Baptist was an ascetic who stressed the Judgment of God. Jesus insisted on forgiveness and love and did not spend his life fasting—some of his adversaries even slandered him as "a glutton and a drunkard" (Matthew 11:19).

To their contemporaries, their messages seemed to be so at odds that in the following decades John the Baptist gathered

disciples of his own, distinct from and even in competition with the early Christians. So if the Gospels from that time speak of the baptism of Jesus, it most likely took place. Yet John the Evangelist's text describes the meeting between Jesus and John the Baptist without even mentioning the baptism itself.

Luke does not say who baptized Jesus, and Matthew omits the fact that John the Baptist baptized for the remission of sins. Because they faced a difficult question: from what possible sin did Jesus need to be saved by baptism? None, obviously.

So why did he need to be baptized? The answer is significant: his baptism was necessary because of his Incarnation. Through his baptism Jesus showed that he had entirely espoused the sinful condition of humanity, even if, personally, he could not sin. He thus expressed how he belonged to the people of Israel that John was urging to return to the path of the Lord. And, in so doing, Jesus sanctioned the acts of John the Baptist.

The Evangelists, however, needed to underscore the fact that Jesus' baptism had a special meaning. So they followed the scene of his baptism with a "theophany," a divine manifestation

that would inspire countless artists. First of all, the heavens opened. For the Hebrews the sky was a solid vault with God on other side. For him to manifest himself, the vault of heaven had to be torn asunder, as told in the books of Isaiah and Ezekiel. But according to the Gospel of Mark, it was Jesus alone who saw the sky being rent. In Mark the entire scene can be interpreted as occurring solely between Jesus and his Father. The skies thus yawned, and, the bond being restored between the dwelling-place of God and the sublunary world, a dove appeared, a manifestation diversely interpreted by specialists. Some see it as the Holy Spirit, but others recall that in Genesis, the first book of the Bible, "the Spirit of the Lord" (his breath), glided over the waters during the creation of the world, like a bird, as if fertilizing the water and creating life.

Then God spoke. For Matthew, he addressed all the witnesses at the scene. For Mark and Luke he spoke to Jesus alone: "You are my beloved Son." In this case, it was a spiritual experience, a vision specific to Jesus. And what did this spiritual experience reveal? The question is a capital one, since for some twenty centuries various specialists, theologians, and exegetes have wondered about the consciousness Jesus might have had of his divine origin at this juncture.

The words lent him by Luke when Mary and Joseph discovered him in the Temple among the doctors when he was twelve: "Did you not know I must be in my Father's house?"(Luke 2:49), seem to indicate that he was already fully aware of his origin as well as his mission. But the thesis has not been universally accepted. It is besides the same Evangelist, Luke, who reports these words of God spoken to Jesus when the heavens opened: "Now it happened that when all the people had been baptized and while Jesus after his own baptism was at prayer, heaven opened and the Holy Spirit descended on him in a physical form, like a dove. And a voice came from heaven, 'You are my Son; today have I fathered you'" (Luke 3:21–22). The same theme is taken up in the Psalms: "I will proclaim the decree of Yahweh: He said to me, 'You are my son, today have I fathered you. Ask of me, and I shall give you the nations as your birthright, the whole wide world as your possession'" (Psa. 2:7–8). For the Jewish people, this expression applied to the long-awaited Messiah. The question then was to emphasize that Jesus was indeed the Messiah. All the more so since some time later John, imprisoned by Herod Antipas, sent an emissary to ask Jesus: "Are you the one who is to come?" (Matt. 11:3). And Jesus answered in the affirmative, quoting his recent miracles and adding: "The good news is proclaimed to the poor, and blessed is anyone who does not find me a cause of falling" (Matt. 11:5–6).

The conclusion is obvious: at the time of his baptism, Jesus gained an acuter, more complete, and clearer conscience of his totally unique relationship to God and of his mission. What occurred on the banks of the Jordan thus becomes clear. It was an announcement to Jesus. This is why the event seemed so crucial to the early Church. At the beginning of the fourth century, January 6 marked the celebration of both the birth and the baptism of Christ. An hymn sung at the time closely linked the two events:

> The whole Creation proclaims it,
> The Magi proclaim it,
> The star proclaims it,
> For see, here is the Son of the King,
> The heavens open,
> The waters of the Jordan foam,
> The dove appears,
> This is my beloved Son.

Later on the two feasts were separated to avoid a confusion deemed heretical: some, in the East especially, claimed that God himself had not been made Man at birth, but had fused himself temporarily with the person of Jesus from the baptism onwards. The Roman Catholic Church condemned this notion at the Council of Nicaea in 353, affirming that Jesus was "true God and true Man," at the moment of his birth.

One thing is undeniable: it was starting with his baptism that Jesus took on his mission; his baptism marked the beginning of his "public life."

And the tester came and said to him, "If you are the Son of God, tell these stones to turn into loaves."
But he replied, "Scripture says, Human beings live not on bread alone but on every word that comes from the mouth of God"

(Matt. 4:3–4).

THE TEMPTATIONS OF JESUS IN THE DESERT

Following his baptism, say the Evangelists Matthew, Mark, and Luke, Jesus withdrew to the desert to pray where he was tested by the devil. The devil is not a common feature in the texts of the Old Testament. Occasionally they do not even seem to regard Satan as fundamentally evil. This is the case in the Book of Job where he belongs to the "court" of Yahweh. But, at the time of Jesus, in the first century, the situation was far different since the Jewish people had become deeply concerned about the misdeeds of this fallen angel. The Gospels thus allude to him frequently and show Jesus as talking about him.

Jesus' stint in the wilderness lasted forty days—a figure not at all chosen at random. The waters of the Flood covered the earth for forty days. David and Solomon each reigned for forty years. The Hebrews' wanderings through the desert on their return from exile in Egypt had the same duration. Moses stayed for forty days and forty nights on Mount Sinai. So many symbols joined together are cause for reflection: the account (which, in Mark, is contained in a single sentence) is probably more theological than historical—not that this makes it any less interesting.

According to Matthew, Jesus was suffering from hunger after fasting for forty days; the devil (the "tester") appeared to him and says: "If you are the Son of God, tell these stones to turn into loaves" (Matt. 4:3). To analyze this first temptation we should compare it with another text of Matthew where the followers of John the Baptist reproached Jesus with the following question: "Why is it that we and the Pharisees fast, but your disciples do not?" (Matt. 9:14). To which Jesus answered: "Surely the bridegroom's attendants cannot mourn as long as the bridegroom is still with them?" (Matt. 9:15). There is thus a close relationship between mourning and fasting, between deprivation of food and the deprivation of the presence of a person. What the devil proposed is that Jesus should wriggle, as it were, out of his predicament, that he should assuage his hunger without worrying about the others. Jesus answered the devil with the Scripture: "Human beings live not on bread alone but on every word that comes from the mouth of God"

Then Jesus was led by the Spirit out into the desert to be put to the test by the devil.

(Matt. 4:1)

(Matt. 4:4). Though this is a biblical quotation, it should be noted that the word is also a privileged means by which people relate to one another—and for Jesus, for God, with man.

The second temptation was set in Jerusalem at the summit of the Temple where the devil had borne Jesus aloft. Indeed all three sites of Jesus' temptation are laden with symbols: first the desert where the Jewish people were tested; then their Temple; and finally the mountain—the one where Moses received the Law, and also Mount Nebo, from where he glimpsed the Promised Land. This time Satan suggested Jesus exert pressure on God by throwing himself from parapet of the Temple, some five hundred feet above the bottom of the ravine of Cedron, so that God would send angels to catch him. The devil clearly knew his Scripture; this was a reference to Psalm 91. And Jesus retorted with an extract from Deuteronomy (a book of the Bible ascribed to Moses but actually written by his followers and which contains the commandments): "Do not put Yahweh your God to the test" (Deut. 6:16).

Not so easily put off, the devil then brought Jesus to the summit of a very high mountain from where all the kingdoms of the world could be seen. He promised to give Jesus sovereignty over all he surveys if he kneels and adores him. Jesus at once replied: "Away with you, Satan!" (Matt. 4:10; this is the celebrated "*Vade retro Satanas*" in the Latin translation, much employed subsequently by the Roman Catholic Church.) Jesus then added a further quotation from Deuteronomy: "Yahweh your God is the one you must fear, him alone you must serve" (Deut. 6:13). Since, it was from God alone that Jesus drew his authority.

The abundance of biblical quotations confirms that this event was a kind of parable, a lesson in theology. Moreover,

since the triple temptation had no witnesses, it must be supposed that Jesus confided it to someone. However, usually when this was the case, the Evangelists made it clear by putting remarks in Jesus' mouth. But there's nothing of the kind here. Why were Matthew and Luke so intent on recording this narrative? Such a story would have hurt rather than helped Jesus' disciples who, after the Resurrection, tried to raise converts. To present Jesus as being subjected to temptation by the devil was unacceptable, indeed scandalous for people of the Jewish faith and many others. But the Evangelists wanted to stress Jesus' human nature, to evoke his inner spiritual battles. They also had to rebuff the adversaries of Jesus who, in a scene from Matthew (12:22–26), reproached his supposed complicity with "Beelzebub, the chief of the devils." After Jesus had cured a "blind and dumb demoniac" the crowd wondered if he could be the "son of David," but his adversaries murmured: "The man drives out devils only through Beelzebub" (with Satan's complicity). Jesus countered with perfect logic that it would be absurd to "drive out Satan" by means of Satan himself.

The account of the three temptations is revealing in another way. It shows what Jesus did not want to be, what he could not be.

To start with, as the first temptation shows, he did not want to be a magician. There were many miracle-workers at this time in the cities and villages of Israel. They employed complicated rituals, cast elaborate and incomprehensible magic spells, earned money, and often pronounced curses (so as to provoke diseases or insomnia, prevent marriages, foment quarrels, and so on). As will be seen, Jesus' miracles were very different. He certainly performed some crowd-pleasing

Next, taking him to a very high mountain, the devil showed him all the kingdoms of the world and their splendor. And he said to him, "I will give you all these if you fall at my feet and do me homage." Then Jesus replied, "Away with you, Satan! For Scripture says: The Lord your God is the one to whom you must do homage, him alone you must serve"

(Matt. 4:8–10).

transformations, as reported by the Gospels. But he did not want anything proved by miracles, even if his companions saw them as evidence of his power, or, as John the Evangelist wrote, as "signs." His strategy was not dependent on the miraculous, on the marvelous; it was in priority addressed to the intelligence of his listeners. This was perhaps the point that Matthew and Luke were trying to get across when they recounted that Jesus refused to transform stones into loaves of bread.

Secondly, Jesus did not want to be king. Both Evangelists wrote as much after his death and Resurrection. And their texts were aimed in priority at the Jewish people, who expected the Messiah to be a king who would drive out the Romans, take power from the emperor, and reign over the entire world. Matthew and Luke thus seem to be saying that Jesus never wanted to be a sovereign of this kind. And therefore he did not "fail."

It is also possible that the temptation story was meant to insinuate something else. To reign over the planet, Jesus would have had to subject himself to the devil, to become his vassal. Could that mean that, in the eyes of the Evangelists, there was something diabolic in all earthly power? It is an involved question, but one from which it is hard to escape.

Finally, the threefold temptation may be given another interpretation. It occurs at the end of forty days of meditation and prayer in the desert. These forty days were not unproductive. At the time of this sojourn in the wilderness—just like for the Jewish people who spent forty years with Moses on their return from Egypt, in a world of rocks and peaks—

greater intimacy was established with God, who ended up dictating his Law and giving instructions to Moses. Moreover he expressed his benevolence to his chosen people by sending manna down upon them: "Something fine and granular, as fine as hoarfrost on the ground." (Ex. 16:14).

Similarly as the Evangelists see it, if Jesus resisted temptation it was because, together with his Father, he had been meditating on his plans for his mission, on what he must be, on what he must do. In this interpretation, the ordeal in the desert marks a new stage after the baptism that further revealed Jesus' personality and mission.

Having left the wilderness and learning of the arrest of John the Baptist, Jesus decided to settle at Capernaum, on the banks of the Lake of Tiberias. It was a small agglomeration on a relatively major road, the Via Maris, which ran from Damascus to the Mediterranean, and recent excavations have revealed traces of it. As it was located on the Galilee border, the Romans, who otherwise did not keep an iron grip on the territory, installed a small garrison, a *centuria* theoretically made up, as the name suggests, of a hundred men, but which at the time of the Gospel probably quartered little more than sixty. With its rows of low dwellings running about half a mile along the bank, the settlement was inhabited by craftsmen who made a living in oil, grapes, and grain from the hinterland, as well as by merchants and fishermen.

It was in Capernaum that Jesus generally resided whenever he was in Galilee. And it was here that he recruited his first companions.

As [Jesus] was walking along by the Lake of Galilee, he saw Simon and Simon's brother Andrew casting a net into the lake—for they were fishermen. And Jesus said to them, "Come after me and I will make you into fishers of people." And at once they left their nets and followed him

(Mark 1:16–18).

CHOOSING THE DISCIPLES

•:•················•:•

The versions of Jesus' beginnings provided by the four Gospels are far from identical. Matthew, Mark, and Luke often tell similar stories. (Their texts are known as the "Synoptic Gospels," from the Greek *sunopsis*, meaning "overview.") They state that he initially preached in Galilee, and eventually arrived in Capernaum, as we have just seen, by traveling on foot and admonishing crowds to repent, "because the Kingdom of God is close at hand" (Mark 1:15; Luke 10:11).

John the Evangelist specifies that shortly after his baptism Jesus again crossed paths with John the Baptist (who obviously did not live at Capernaum) accompanied by two of his disciples, Andrew and another unknown. On advice from John the Baptist, they followed Jesus. "Jesus turned round, saw them following and said, 'What do you want?' They answered, 'Rabbi'—which means Teacher," and spent the day with him (John 1:38). The following day or even that very evening, a chain was already being forged. Andrew ran off to look for his brother Simon (Peter), to tell him the news that they had discovered the Messiah. Then the same Andrew went to find one of his friends—thereafter they are often shown acting

together—named Philip. Philip in his turn met Nathanael, who was reticent at first, since Jesus came from Nazareth, a village that seemed to have had a bad reputation. "From Nazareth?" he said, "Can anything good come from that place?" (John 1:46). But Jesus told Nathanael that he already knew him—he had seen him earlier under a fig tree, before Philip had called him. According to tradition, the fig tree was regarded as the tree of knowledge of happiness and misfortune. Jesus' strange expression thus seems to mean that in studying the Law Nathanael had been preparing himself to meet him. In any case, Nathanael was completely overcome, to the point of immediately proclaiming Jesus to be King of Israel. Jesus calmed him down: "You believe that just because I said: I saw you under the fig tree. You are going to see greater things than that." In other words, this was only the beginning.

This episode in John's Gospel raises a question: it is the only point in any of the Gospels in which Nathanael's name is cited. He is not found, in particular, in the list of the twelve apostles. On the other hand, Bartholomew, who is always indicated in the list, appears nowhere else in the New Testament. Some

*As Jesus was walking out from there, he saw a man named Matthew sitting at the tax office
and said to him, "Follow me." And he got up and followed him*

(Matt. 9:9).

have tried to see Nathanael and Bartholomew as one and the same, but there is no indication that this is the case. We can thus suppose that Nathanael, a disciple, was not actually an apostle, and that the distinction between the apostles and other disciples is far from always being clear-cut. One point is certain: the word "disciple" is employed throughout the New Testament to mean only those who accompanied Jesus, and not, for example, the earliest converts. According to the Gospels of Matthew, Mark, and Luke, it was in Capernaum that Jesus saw Simon (whom he would rename Peter) and Andrew busy casting their nets. They were not originally from the city but from Bethsaida, a small town located farther to the north on the other side of the lake. Perhaps they settled at Capernaum because, on this bank, there were many small locales for smoking or salting fish, which was then sold all over the region. One of best of these fish was *Zeus faber,* now known as John Dory—and in Latin languages "Saint Peter."

Mark's text quotes a now famous saying of Jesus addressed to Peter and Andrew: "Come after me and I will make you into fishers of people" (Mark 1:17). This expression does not appear in the Old Testament, later in the Gospels, nor even in Christian writings of the first two centuries. The fishing metaphor, however, was frequent throughout the Mediterranean Basin, given the importance of this particular trade. It could be concluded that in speaking in this way Jesus wanted to confer on Peter and Andrew an especially eminent role.

They joined him at once. All three walked passed Zebedee, toiling away with his two sons, James and John, and other workmen. Jesus called the sons, still young surely since they were not yet working independently. He gave them the name

"Boanerges," a term cobbled together from Aramaic, Hebrew, and Greek, and which would have been the despair of linguists had Mark not obligingly provided a translation: "sons of thunder" (Mark 3:17). But the difficulty is barely dispelled: why the nickname? Supposing that the two boys might have possessed loud voices, most specialists assume that they were of boisterous temperament. Neither did their mother lack personality: she insisted that Jesus should bestow a good position on her sons when he became king.

As time went on, the small group grew—some of them, as mentioned earlier, were John the Baptist's former disciples. According to Mark, it was still in the same region that Jesus called forth Levi "son of Alpheus." The Evangelist Matthew called him Levi-Matthew. But they were not one and the same person, as was long thought. Levi-Matthew was a very different sort of character from the first four. He was a "publican," that is, a tax collector—a much-hated profession. Publicans worked as much for Herod Antipas as for the Romans. They were so detested, in fact, that the Pharisees reproached Jesus for eating "with tax collectors and sinners" (Mark 2:16). (Members of an influential sect, the Pharisees observed the Law rigorously, in particular to protect Jewish identity in a spirit of resistance to the Romans; in their opinion, a tax collector was a kind of "collaborator.")

The fact that Jesus called Levi to follow him, shows that he paid no attention to the prevailing politico-religious system, a tendency that made him highly suspect in the eyes of the authorities. He chose his men from all walks of life: conformist peasants and less appreciated fishermen alike; Galileans and at least one man from Judea (Judas); a tax collector; and opponents of the government, such as Simon. These young men did

So now I say to you: "You are Peter and on this rock I will build my community. And the gates of the underworld can never overpower it. I will give you the keys of the Kingdom of Heaven"

(Matt. 16:18–19).

not always get along, being envious and wary of one another, and Jesus was often obliged to call them to order. And yet they would follow him to the last day, abandoning everything for him (even if one or two went home to see wife and children or to help bring in the harvest). They shared everything with him, hunger—and some good meals too—triumph, hostility, and finally exhaustion. Around them gathered a second wider circle of disciples or sympathizers. Luke notes that when Jesus went up to Jerusalem he was preceded by an avant-garde of missionaries enjoined to announce the kingdom of God: "the Lord appointed seventy-two others [other than, the apostles] and sent them out ahead of him in pairs, to all the towns and places he himself would be visiting" (Luke 10:1).

The figure of seventy-two should not be taken literally because it corresponds to that of the "nations of the world" which, in the words of Genesis, sprang from the sons of Noah. But it does mean that the disciples, or sympathizers, were numerous. Such terminological questions are far from cut and dried: how, for example, should Lazarus, a close friend of Jesus, who lodged in his house, be classified?

From the time he recruited his more active companions, in any case, Jesus asked that they follow him without hesitation; one was not given the time to alert his family and another could not attend his father's funeral (Luke 9:59–62; Matt. 8:21–22). Sometimes Jesus was rebuffed. The most famous case is that of a wealthy young man, well disposed towards him, whom Jesus held in affection; but the youth refused to follow Jesus because he would have to abandon all his worldly goods, of which he had many.

Jesus was fully conscious of just how cutting this was. Moreover, even his own family was divided on the point. But, following the refusal of the rich youth, he said to Peter and the others: "In truth I tell you, there is no one who has left house, brothers, sisters, mother, father, children or land . . . who will not receive a hundred times as much . . . and, in the world to come, eternal life" (Mark 10:29–30).

Women too followed Jesus. Luke mentions "Mary, surnamed the Magdalene, from whom seven demons had gone out, Joanna, the wife of Herod's steward Chuza, and Susanna, and many others who provided for them out of their own resources" (Luke 8:1–3). Unlike the men, they were not called by Jesus, but were nonetheless accepted and admitted together with his companions, even if they were not numbered among the Twelve (the number of the tribes of Israel). When Luke wrote that Mary Magdalene had been exorcised of seven demons (the sacred figure recalls the account in Genesis of the Creation and stands for plenitude), he meant that she had been cured by Jesus of a serious disease of some unspecified nature. As for Joanna, so often ignored or passed over, she most probably appeared as one of the first to help Jesus and his close associates with their "resources." Still it is easy to imagine the risks they ran for their reputations. The fact that Jesus surrounded himself with women (something that has fuelled the imaginations of a host of novelists) signaled a minor revolution at the time. By the time that the Acts of the Apostles were written (mainly by Luke), recounting the formation of the earliest Christian communities, the women had disappeared.

John the Baptist

According to Luke, John the Baptist began baptizing, "In the fifteenth year of Tiberius Caesar's reign" (Luke 3:1). Experts on the Roman calendar calculate that this "fifteenth year" had begun on December 10, 27 CE.

Nothing is known of John's life up to this point, except for one point: he must have refused the priesthood. The priesthood, in fact, was hereditary. He should therefore have succeeded his father, the old priest Zacharias, and entered the class of Abbia (the priestly community was divided into twenty-four classes, that of Abbia being the eighth, an honorable rank). John's refusal was thus an early pointer to his break with the sacerdotal caste, with the Temple of Jerusalem.

It has sometimes been supposed that he had been brought up among the Essenians, many of whom lived in the desert in an ascetic manner, like him. This might have been all the more feasible since, according to the historian Flavius Josephus, the Essenians often adopted children to indoctrinate them. But would Zacharias, belonging to the sacerdotal caste, readily have entrusted his son to a people so hostile to his own? And finally John's baptism had little in common with the practice among the Essenians. Such an assumption can thus be rejected.

After Jesus began preaching (and, initially, baptizing too), John did not join him, but continued his mission separately, surrounded by his own disciples. Mark described the death of John the Baptist at some length (Mark 6:17–29) in an account which has greatly inspired artists and writers. According to Mark, John had reproached Herod Antipas for repudiating his first wife in order to marry Herodias, ex-wife of one of his half-brothers. Following this criticism Antipas had the prophet arrested. Then one wine-filled evening, the tetrarch of Galilee was so delighted by the dancing of Salome, the daughter of Herodias, that he promised to give her anything she asked for. The girl demanded the severed head of John the Baptist and it was promptly brought to her on a platter.

As Mark related it, however, the account is riddled with historical and geographical errors. Still, it is known that John the Baptist, a holy man many venerated after his death as a martyr, was assassinated on orders from Herod Antipas. The scene can be seen viewed as a prefiguration of the death of Jesus. Learning of John's fate, Christ was all the more aware of the risks he himself was running.

LAMBERT SUSTRIS, *THE BAPTISM OF CHRIST*, 1552.
MUSÉE DES BEAUX-ARTS, CAEN.

In the Wilderness

In the Bible, the word wilderness (the desert) has two senses: a place, of course, but also a time.

The desert is naturally a type of landscape designated by geographers: an almost uninhabited area, where springs are rare and vegetation meager. At the time Palestine was fertile and well cultivated (it was the Ottoman occupation, especially in the nineteenth century, that laid it to waste). But the desert was very close. When Jesus questioned his listeners as to what they would do if a sheep wandered off from the fold, it was assumed that the animal would wander into the desert. The desert of Judea where John the Baptist lived corresponded to the eastern slope of the region's mountains, towards the valley of the Jordan and the Dead Sea.

Symbolically, the desert, the wilderness in the Bible, was also a land which God had not blessed, in which evil spirits took refuge, as can be seen from the book of Isaiah. Matthew quotes these words of Jesus: "When an unclean spirit goes out of someone, it wanders through waterless country looking for a place to rest and cannot find one" (Matt. 12:43).

On the other hand, the desert can be also a place of prayer. Mark in his Gospel tells us that Jesus, the day after he had cured the mother-in-law of Peter, "got up and left the house and went off to a lonely place, and prayed there" (Mark 1:35). Solitude makes it possible—though not always—to come nearer to God.

In the Old Testament, the desert was often a refuge: David went there to flee the wrath of King Saul who, jealous of his triumphs, wanted to kill him; in the same way the prophet Elijah took flight before the anger of Queen Jezebel, a pagan who had designs of fostering the cult of the god Baal on Israel.

But in the Old Testament the wilderness was more especially a crucial period in sacred history. It is there that Yahweh appeared to Moses and his people, Israel. And, reproaching this "perverse community" (Num. 14:27) for constantly rebelling against him, he imposed a penitence, which also served as a period of reflection and meditation that lasted forty years.

At the end of this harsh training period, Moses built a "Tent of Meeting" in which he dialogued with God. In the end, Yahweh had him inscribe his laws on two stone tablets, so forging a new Covenant with Israel. The wilderness thus stands for the long march towards God.

Peter

Of all the companions of Jesus, Peter is the most frequently mentioned in the texts, the most actively committed, and thus the most significant. He was a fisherman, married and with children, who resided at Capernaum, a fishing port and a relatively important town.

In 1986, on the shore of the Lake of Tiberias, a thirty-three-foot-long wooden boat was dug out of the mud. Carbon-14 dating and other indications established that it was some two thousand years old and it provided insights into the conditions under which the fishermen of the Lake exercised their trade. Taking into account its length, it would have needed five oarsmen to power it. Note also that, in the Gospels, Peter was not alone when recruited by Jesus. According to Mark, he was called at the same time as his brother Andrew and immediately before James and John, the two sons of an important fishing-boat owner.

If Peter is regarded as the first of the apostles, it is because he appears in all four Gospels—they are unanimous on this point—as their spokesman and chief. The four texts also state that he was nicknamed Képà in Aramaic (Kephas in Greek, which became, still in Greek, Petros), a name meaning "rock" or "stone." "You are Peter, and on this rock I will build my community," Jesus told him so as to make clear the primacy of Peter over the other apostles (Matt. 16:18). It is to Peter that Jesus gave the keys to the kingdom of heaven (Matt. 16:19).

The Gospels also report that Peter, present at the Last Supper eaten by Jesus with his companions, followed him after his arrest at Gethsemane to the place where he was arraigned before the high priest. But, recognized by a maidservant (apparently because of his Galilean accent), he denied being a disciple of Jesus and fled.

After the Resurrection, his ascendancy over the other companions became abundantly clear. He spoke in front of crowds in Jerusalem and announced the Christian Messiah. After being imprisoned, he left Jerusalem and Palestine to spread "the good news" in Antioch and perhaps in Corinth. According to the Gospel of John, he was martyred. This would have occurred in Rome, according to certain texts by the early Fathers of the Church, in particular Saint Clement, bishop of the capital of the Empire at the end of first century.

Excavations in the mid-twentieth century have led some to surmise that that he might be interred in a necropolis located in the hill of the Vatican, under the basilica that bears his name.

THE MESSAGE

Look, I shall send my messenger to clear a way before me. And suddenly the Lord you seek will come to his Temple; yes the angel of the covenant for whom you long, is on his way, says Yahweh Sabaoth. Who will be able to resist the day of his coming? Who will remain standing when he appears? For he will be like a refiner's fire, like fuller's alkali (Mal. 3:1—2).

But such large crowds gathered around him that he got into a boat and sat there. The people all stood on the shore

(Matt. 13:2).

JESUS STARTS TO PREACH

•:⋯⋯⋯⋯:•

One particular Sabbath proved an amazing day for the inhabitants of Nazareth. They had gathered together, as usual, at the synagogue. Jesus had apparently already begun to preach in the region, and the peasants and olive-growers who had come to the service knew it. But what they were about to hear was to astonish them beyond all measure, and, in the final analysis, it outraged them.

The person in charge of the synagogue, according to custom, was to choose a man among those able to read an extract from the Scriptures. Seeing Jesus, he pointed to him. Standing up, Jesus unrolled the book of the prophet Isaiah and read the passage where it is written: "The spirit of Lord Yahweh is on me for Yahweh has anointed me. He has sent me to bring the news to the afflicted, to soothe the brokenhearted, to proclaim liberty to captives, release to those in prison, to proclaim a year of favor from Yahweh and a day of vengeance for our God" (Is. 61:1–2).

This text concerns the envoy of God considered as the Messiah for whom the Jewish people had been waiting.

Concluding, Jesus sat down and said to them: "This text is being fulfilled today even while you are listening" (Luke 4:21). This—after some hesitation according to Luke—they were unwilling to countenance. How dare the son of Joseph, the son of Mary, this carpenter, proclaim himself as having been sent by God? They refused to listen to him any longer and Jesus went on his way, returning to Capernaum where he preached again. "And his teaching made a deep impression on them because his word carried authority" (Luke 4:32).

And what exactly did he preach? He announced "the kingdom of God"—the expression appears only once in the Old Testament, but it returns unceasingly in Christ's teachings. A kingdom to come, which was already mysteriously present, since he, Jesus, was before them.

"The coming of the kingdom of God does not admit of observation . . . For look, the kingdom of God is among you" (Luke 17:20–21). At the same time, Jesus taught his companions "The Lord's Prayer" or "Our Father," in which the

faithful beseech God using the words "thy kingdom come."
Thus this kingdom was already there on that day, but it would
be greater thereafter, more universal, joining within it people
of nations other than Jewish people.

And how would it appear, this kingdom? Jesus answered
by the famous text of the Beatitudes:

> Blessed are you who are poor: the kingdom of God is
> yours. Blessed are you who are hungry now; you shall
> have your fill.
> Blessed are you who are weeping now: you shall laugh.
> Blessed are you, when people hate you, drive you out,
> abuse you, denounce your name as criminal on account
> of the Son of Man (Luke 6, 20–22).

This was the world turned upside-down. Those who heard
these words understood that they described a society completely different from their own, that they spoke of a king
who did things that earthly kings neglected: defended wid-
ows and orphans, safeguarded the oppressed, took care that
justice was done.

The great prophets of the Old Testament, Amos and Hosea,
for example, had certainly criticized the material conditions of
their time. Thus, Amos, in the eighth century BCE, denounced
the cruel treatment of prisoners of war and the sale of the poor
for the slightest involvement in debt. But Jesus' message was
far more general; he announced a new type of society, a happy
one, a "heavenly banquet" in which—the fact bears repeating—peoples of nations other than the Jewish one would take
part in the company of the patriarchs of Israel. And it is no
coincidence that Luke, almost immediately after quoting the
Beatitudes, told the story of the Roman centurion.

As we have seen, the Romans maintained a light garrison
at Capernaum. When Jesus entered the town, the commanding officer came up to him and told him that his servant (or
son according to certain translations) was sick and close to
death. Having heard speak of the cures Jesus performed, he

The centurion replied, "Sir, I am not worthy to have you under my roof; just give the word and my servant will be cured"
(Matt. 8:8).

"Whoever drinks this water will be thirsty again; but no one who drinks the water that I shall give will ever be thirsty again: the water I shall give will become a spring of water within, welling up for eternal life"

(John 4:13–14).

had called upon some Jewish elders to act as intermediaries, which they did. Jesus accepted the task and was near the man's house when the centurion sent word to him, saying that Jesus should not put himself to the trouble of coming in person, but rather "let my boy be cured by your giving the word" (Luke 7:7). (The phrase is still repeated during the Roman Catholic Mass shortly before the faithful take Communion: "Say but the word and my soul shall be healed.") After receiving this message from the centurion, the Gospel tells us, Jesus was "astonished at him" and said to those near him: "I tell you, not even in Israel have I found faith as great as this" (Luke 7:9). In this way, of course, it was emphasized that outsiders could also believe in the God that Jesus proclaimed. And the patient was cured.

John the Evangelist recounts more or less the same story, not of a centurion but of a "royal official," and the scene was located not in Capernaum but at Cana. This time, Jesus did not admire the official's strength of belief, but stressed that faith, and that only, was required for salvation. But it was still a heathen, once again, who benefited.

The kingdom, then, was open to all. Even to the Samaritans, who were sworn enemies of the orthodox Jews. They shared a common origin but had been at loggerheads for ancient and very complicated reasons, which were deeply entrenched. So much so that the Samaritans, excluded from the Temple, had built one of their own on Mount Garizim. This Temple had been razed in the second century BCE, but the Samaritans continued to worship on the Mount. As history has too often shown, people can believe in the same God yet scorn or hate one another. For the Jews of Judea and Galilee being a Samaritan was equivalent to being a pagan, or even possessed by a demon. In traveling from Galilee to Judea, they would avoid passing through Samaria. They were not always wrong to be worried. Luke tells of how one day, shortly before the arrest of Jesus, he wanted to pause with his disciples in a Samaritan village, but lodging was refused to them "because he was making for Jerusalem" (Luke 9:51–53).

Another time, however, when in an exhausted state they were proceeding in the opposite direction, from Judea towards Galilee, Jesus sat down by a well while his compan-

ions went off to glean some provisions in the neighborhood (John 4:1–26). A woman of Samaria approached and he asked her to give him something to drink. She could hardly believe her ears. He, a Jew, spoke to her, and requested water of her? He answered: "If only you knew what God is offering" (John 4:10), letting it be known that he had a special relation to the divine. He thus infringed on three taboos. The pride of a Jewish man should not have permitted him to ask assistance from a Samaritan. In addition, it was utterly beneath a man to ask anything of a woman. Lastly, he had spoken of religious questions with someone whose faith his own people disparaged. Many would have refused. But not Jesus. Then he spoke of water that of itself was "living water," the revelation of the true God. Next he teased the woman, asking her to call forth her husband, but she replied that she did not have one. This he knew and answered back: "You are right to say, I have no husband; for although you have had five, the one you have now is not your husband" (John 4:17–18).

That was a strange dialogue, all the more so since only three successive marriages were allowed. Some have claimed that this was only an allegory and that the five "husbands" corresponded to the five gods introduced in Samaria by the Assyrians in the eighth century BCE. But this explanation is surely too complicated for readers of the Gospel of John at that time. It is also possible to see this move from one husband to another as the expression of a search, of a quest for truth by a woman forever disappointed, never satisfied. Jesus' answer finally made her feel understood.

Subsequently, the conversation was no more about husbands but about faith. She called Jesus a "prophet" and questioned him: the Samaritans adored God on Mount Garizim and the Jews in Jerusalem. What should she believe? What should she do? The response was twofold. First point: salvation came from the Jews (the name of Israel is not written). Second and crucial point: "the hour is coming— indeed is already here—when true worshippers will worship the Father in spirit and truth" (John 4:23). In other words, Jesus told her that she now knew the truth about God who is the Father. She should seek no more. Revelation was there.

His mother said to the servants, "Do whatever he tells you"
(John 2:5).

THE MIRACLES

•:⋯⋯⋯⋯⋯⋯:•

The Gospels record forty miracles by Jesus. They are, however, not always the same ones: among the seven that John recounts, for instance, six (some of the most famous, including Cana) are not found in the three other texts. But all imply that Jesus performed other miraculous interventions, "many," as John put it (John 20:30).

Most of the time, he cured the sick: the blind, the paralytic, lepers, and deaf-mutes. In other cases he overcame natural laws: calming a storm or multiplying bread and fishes in the desert.

According to the Gospels, Jesus' attitude with regard to his miracles seems ambiguous. When John the Baptist sent emissaries to ask him whether he was truly "he who must come," he answered by referring to his miracles. But he did not like to perform them in a spectacular or impressive manner. Mark recalls how one day he was brought "one that was deaf, and had an impediment in his speech," and Jesus "took him aside" to cure him (Mark 7:32–36). Similarly, when in Bethesda he was presented with a blind man whom he was requested to

touch, he led him out into the fields, cured him, and sent home asking him not even "to go into the village" (Mark 8:26). And when a leper threw himself down in front of him, beseeching him to be assuaged, which he was, Jesus said "mind you tell no one anything" (Mark 1:44), though it was an injunction the leper failed to follow.

Ascribing miracles to Jesus must have surprised his contemporaries less than it does readers today. In the synagogue, the faithful had regularly heard speak of the parting of the Red Sea for their ancestors fleeing Egypt and they had been told of the walls of Jericho collapsing—not from military action but as a result of prayer, at the sound of the trumpets of the people led by Joshua. In the main, the miracles of Jesus were less spectacular than these.

The Gospels, however, are tireless in their account of his cures, acts to which the first Christian communities attached great importance. Moreover according to the Acts of the Apostles, on the day of Pentecost, Peter declared to those present that God had "commended" Jesus to them "by the

Then Jesus spoke, "What do you want me to do for you?" The blind man said to him, "Rabbuni, let me see again."
Jesus said to him, "Go: your faith has saved you." And at once his sight returned and he followed him along the road
(Mark 10:51–52).

miracles and portents and signs that God worked through him" (Acts 2:22). The word "commended" is highly significant: for the men and women whom Peter addressed, no one could be taken for a prophet if he was not at the same time a miracle worker.

Of course, the historical reality of these cures has stirred up great controversy. Today, many historians recognize that Jesus was a true healer and a number of episodes recall the medical practice of the time. For instance, John tells of the meeting between Jesus and a man blind from birth near the Temple in Jerusalem: Jesus "spat on the ground, and made a paste with the spittle, and put this over the eyes of the blind man," and he was cured (John 9:1–7). The use of saliva in the treatment of eye ailments was relatively frequent in this period.

Some have wondered whether some accounts of the miracles were not originally parables transformed little by little as they were told from Christian to Christian after Jesus' departure. This might explain the strange episode of the fig tree that a hungry Jesus on the road found to bear no fruit, a hardly sur-

prising occurrence since the scene took place in springtime, as Mark, who tells the story, makes clear: "For it was not the season for figs" (Mark 11:13). Nonetheless, Jesus condemned the fig tree and next time he passed by the tree had withered and died. In fact, the story was about Israel, which was to be condemned since it failed to produce the fruits Jesus expected of it (the episode took place at a time of great tension between Jesus and the Temple).

Jesus performed other, more spectacular miracles. For example, the resurrection of Lazarus, told only in the Gospel of John (11:1–45). Though the text is of massive theological significance, can it be rooted in historical fact? It should be noted straightaway that this resurrection is not to be compared to that of Jesus, since Lazarus was to die thereafter; but it should be conceded, even if it is hard for rationalist minds, that Jesus certainly performed astounding acts that impressed the people. Most specialists believe that the story of this resurrection has its remote source in a traditional tale of the period—based on a man who came back to life—onto which

"Sir, I have no one to put me into the pool when the water is disturbed; and while I am still on the way, someone else gets down there before me"

(John 5:7).

John the Evangelist grafted a multifaceted theological lesson.

The prefiguration of the resurrection of Jesus, of his victory over death, is obvious. Moreover, as Saint Iraeneus, bishop of Lyon, already noted at the beginning of the third century: "The dead man goes off, hands and feet bound in bandages: this is a symbol for Man hobbled by sin." And it is Jesus who untied him. He was the liberator. He washed away sin.

But the essence of the narrative does not lie in the resurrection, it lies in Jesus' dialog with Martha, Lazarus' sister when he arrived at Bethany. Christ says: "Anyone who believes in me, even though that person dies, will live" (John 11:25). And Martha answered that she believed Jesus to be the Christ, "the Son of God" (John 11:27). This is all that need be said.

Jesus himself often emphasized that the significant thing was not always the event in itself but the teaching to be drawn from it, as he made clear in reference to the miracle of the loaves and the fishes. The story is well known. Thousands of people had followed Jesus into a nearby desert to hear him, see him, touch him, perhaps even to ask him to cure them. Evening drew in. The disciples would have been prepared to send the people away to look for food and rest elsewhere, but Jesus busied himself getting them something to eat. But how? The apostle Andrew noticed that a boy in the crowd had brought with him five barley loaves and two fishes. To feed four or five thousand people with that was obviously absurd. But Jesus set to, taking the loaves and, having "given thanks," handed them out to the crowd, just like a good Jewish father presiding over the evening meal and thanking the Lord before serving the food. And there was enough for everyone, with even twelve baskets of leftovers (twelve like the twelve tribes of Israel, twelve like the apostles). At this point the crowd acclaimed Jesus as "the prophet who is to come into the world" (John 6:14). Not *a* prophet among others but *the* prophet, the future king of Israel, a kind of political-religious sovereign. Loath to accept, Jesus withdrew to the mountains, alone.

The narrative is, of course, peppered with symbols. Thus, the figure of five loaves and two fishes is no coincidence: there are five books of the Law, supplemented by the "scriptures" and the "prophets" represented by the two fish. But Jesus "multiplied" the lessons of these scriptures, just as he did with the bread, so that it could provide greater sustenance. Moreover, these tales come before the Last Supper Jesus takes with his disciples before his arrest at which he would call the bread his body.

The Evangelists' accounts of this fabulous meal only run to a few lines since they are more interested in what follows. Jesus withdrew to the mountains with the crowd on his trail. Finally, they found him. He explained that his task was to afford them a different kind of bread. Not all of them believed it. As John's Gospel tells us: "After this, many of his disciples went away and accompanied him no more" (John 6:66). Christ spoke of another kingdom and, in a very long speech, explained why he was the bread of life that guaranteed eternal life to those who believed in him. One thing is clear: a miracle, be it impressive or not, possessed two meanings. It cast lights on Jesus' compassion for those who suffer and who are hungry. But it was also a "sign" (this is the very word John employs) intended to transmit the message.

He gave orders that the people were to sit down on the grass; then he took the five loaves and the two fish, raised his eyes to heaven and said the blessing. And breaking the loaves he handed them to his disciples who gave them to the crowds

(Matt. 14:19).

He took with him Peter and James and John and went up the mountain to pray. And it happened that,
as he was praying, the aspect of his face was changed and his clothing became sparkling white
(Luke 9:28–29).

RAPHAEL. *THE TRANSFIGURATION*. 1518–20.
PINACOTECA, VATICAN MUSEUMS, ROME.

PARABLES THAT EXPLAIN WHO GOD IS

•:·················:•

One day, Luke informs us, Jesus spoke at length, delivering a crucial lesson. He had been invited on the Sabbath day to take the meal with one of the "chiefs of the Pharisees" (something that shows that his relations with them were not always so strained). He spoke to the crowd, expressing himself primarily in parables.

Rabbis often employed parables in their teachings. In the Gospels, they generally took the form of little stories or just a few words designed to give greater force to the message of Jesus. They were intended to offer listeners a better understanding of the nature of God, but also to make them undergo a radical change and repent. This did not mean they were expected to live in perpetual remorse or be complacent in their feelings of guilt, but rather, they should change course, change direction in their lives, and conform to the will of God.

On that day, according to Luke (15:4–32), Jesus told three parables that many theologians regard as particularly precious. The first concerns a lost sheep: a shepherd watched over a flock of a hundred; one of them vanished; worried, he left the ninety-nine others in the wilderness and sallied forth to look for it; and when he found it, he called on his entourage, friends, and neighbors to celebrate its return with him. "In the same way, I tell you, there will be more rejoicing in heaven over one sinner repenting than over ninety-nine upright people who have no need of repentance" (Luke 15:7). In other words, for Jesus, the lost sheep was one who was not righteous and did not observe the law of love, that love that extends to enemies: "Love your enemies, do good to those who hate you" (Luke 6:27). This does not mean, of course, that "enemies" should be allowed to perform evil acts.

The second story Jesus relayed is very similar. It tells of a woman who mislaid a silver coin—not just anyone but one with which wives adorned their foreheads. Representing her dowry, it was never to be taken off, even at night. So the woman set to with her broom and swept the whole house. Here, Jesus did not talk about the fear that would have gripped

FACING PAGE

REMBRANDT, *THE PARABLE OF THE RICH MAN*, 1627.
GEMÄLDEGALERIE, BERLIN.

FOLLOWING PAGE

PALMA GIOVANE, *THE RETURN OF THE PRODIGAL SON*, 1605.
GALLERIA DELL'ACCADEMIA, VENICE.

the wife: what would her husband say? At long last, with relief and joy, she found the coin. Her joy too had to be shared with friends and neighbors. Jesus often, indeed very often, spoke of joy, much more than of suffering and pain. What he announced was joy, since for him suffering was not good.

There was again a question of joy in the third story—the richest in meaning and the most famous—that of the prodigal son. A rich landowner had two sons. At the time this would have been very few since the Jewish people regarded having many children as a sign of divine favor. But apparently Jesus was only interested in comparing the attitudes of the two brothers. The younger son asked his father for "the share of the estate that will come to me" (Luke 15:12). It was a hurtful request, not only because it would upset the balance of the family but also because usually the estate was divided only at the death of the father or at least at his initiative. The father did his son's bidding, however, without objection or discussion. He entirely respected the son's freedom, just as God does with man. And this is the parable's first lesson.

Jesus' audience was made up of country folk. Even if they all were not farmers or landowners, they all knew the problem a son's attitude could pose for the management of their property. Even if, according to the law of the time, the younger son had a right only to one third of the inheritance, the estate was comprised essentially of land and livestock. But this son did not want it, because he had decided to leave and take his money with him. To rustle up such a sum, "in cash,"

and quickly, was at the very least irritating. And every one of Jesus' listeners was well aware of this.

So the son departed, dreaming of living his own life with the money he had received. Very quickly he spent all he had, "on a life of debauchery" as Jesus put it (Luke 15:13), that many have read as meaning sumptuous meals, gambling, wild parties, and so on. Soon the cupboard was bare and, it seems, even his companions forsake him. A rich man has but fair-weather friends. So the boy was left alone, without a penny, in a far country where there occurred a severe famine and a serious economic crisis. The spendthrift sought work, and found it with a big landowner who sets him to keep the pigs.

Pigs! For a Jew, this was the most ghastly animal that existed. Deuteronomy, one of the most significant books of the Bible, even forbids the touching of a pig's corpse (Deut. 14:8). Such was the abasement, shame, and sin to which the youth was reduced. Still more, he was not even allowed to partake of the pig swill. His initial reaction was self-centered: he compared his situation with that enjoyed by his father's workmen who had "all the food they want and more" (Luke 15:17). He thus decided to make his way home; but he has changed and so steels himself to admit to his father that he has sinned "against heaven and against you" (Luke 15:18). On the road, he rehearsed his plea for forgiveness: "I no longer deserve to be called your son; treat me as one of your hired men" (Luke 15:19). He could not hope, he could not even dare to wish to be restored to his former position, but he

"My soul, you have plenty of good things laid by for many years to come. Take things easy, eat, drink, have a good time." But God said to him, "Fool! This very night the demand will be made for your soul; and this hoard of yours, whose will it be then?"

(Luke 12:19–20).

But a Samaritan traveler who came on him was moved by compassion
(Luke 10:33).

started up, not knowing how he would be received. Still he did not expect to actually be rejected. He now had confidence. And a little faith.

His father—God, of course—saw him arriving from afar. So he had been waiting, watching for him. He recognized him in spite of the distance and was already rejoicing, for his son was alive. The father had no idea of his son's intentions. After all, it was possible that he was just coming back to scrounge more money. But seeing his ragged clothing, his downcast look, the father "was moved with pity" or "felt compassion"; such are the terms employed in the majority of the translations of this Gospel. Several specialists have pointed out that the Greek word *esplagknisthe* evokes a deeper feeling, a "stirring of the entrails," a total upheaval, just as when people say of some exceptional occurrence that it "quickened the blood."

Overwhelmed, the father ran out to this beggar and embraced him. It was only then that the son expressed his regret: forgiveness preceded acknowledgment and confession.

Jesus did not even say that the father demanded further explanation from his repentant son, but he at once ordered the finest garment be brought (to dress someone in a long robe was to honor him), that a ring be placed on his finger (a sign of authority), and that a feast be prepared. Now the son,

as is clear, had performed no worthy deed. On the contrary, if he had returned, it was because he was urged on by necessity. But a banquet would be held, as the father says, "because this son of mine was dead and has come back to life" (Luke 15:24). He was "dead": separation from God meant death. But God forgets it as soon as one begins to walk with him. He is not very demanding.

The elder son who had stayed with his father and toiled in the fields was disgusted by the reception given his brother. Never, he said to his father, have you ever given me anything "to celebrate with my friends. But, for this son of yours..." (Luke 15:29–30). The elder son had, however, lost nothing. The father answered him, calm and joyous: "My son, you are with me always and all I have is yours" (Luke 15:31). His love was big enough for two, for three. For all.

One error in interpretation is to be avoided. The father's attitude—that of God—does not mean man is permitted to do anything. In Jesus' words recorded by the Gospels, there are thirty allusions to judgment. But, if one examines them closely, in nearly every case, forgiveness is offered prior to judgment and judgment comes only if man rejects forgiveness or grace. Because man is responsible for his acts. He is not a child to whom one can turn a blind eye.

Cana

The miracle of Cana is well known: Jesus met his mother at a wedding to which he was invited. She told him the guests had no more wine to drink. Having first stated that this was none of his business, he gave in and ordered some servants present to fill six empty stone jars with water. The contents immediately turned into wine and very fine wine at that. The significant thing in the account of this miracle, which is found only in John's Gospel (2:1–12), is not the transformation of the water into wine but the symbols that spring from it. Long before, classical Antiquity had established an equivalence between what it called the sap of the vine and the blood running in the vessels of men and animals. Pressed and crushed, bunches of grapes turn into scarlet blood. They pass though a kind of death before being reborn differently. In the same way, Jesus gave wine to his disciples and told them that it was his blood—after his death he returned differently.

What wedding was this in point of fact? Oddly enough, the bride did not appear in the story. The leading role was played by Mary, who was not designated by her name but as "the mother of Jesus." Many specialists aware that John the Evangelist was fond of speaking in symbols, are of the opinion that here "the mother of Jesus" stands for Israel, and read the miracle as follows: Israel observed her distress (the shortage of wine) but Jesus did not immediately answer it because his mission was of greater breadth: it was universal. But Israel was not for all that discouraged: "His mother said to the servants. 'Do whatever he tells you'" (John 2:5). Then Jesus accepted. And when the servants trusted and obeyed, the water they poured into the jars turned into a new wine, better than the preceding. Jesus brought a more complete, total revelation of God. Thanks to him, the New Covenant (a new wedding) between God and man could be celebrated.

GIOTTO, *THE WEDDING AT CANA*.
C. 1303–05.
CAPPELLA DEI SCROVEGNI, PADUA.

The Pharisees

The Gospels, especially those of Matthew and John, present a very negative view of the Pharisees, seen as unrelenting adversaries of Jesus, ever suspicious, liars even. This is because by the time these texts were written, after the destruction of the Temple by the Romans in the year 70, the Pharisees had supplanted the caste of high priests (the Sadducees) and then represented the principal religious authority with which the first Christian communities were often in violent conflict. On this point, you cannot regard the Evangelists as "unbiased" observers.

The sect of the Pharisees had appeared in the second century BCE. They wanted to fight against the cultural hegemony of Greece, which they saw as liable to distort Judaism and they strove to maintain the cohesion of the people in the face of the Romans. They thus insisted on the thorough study and meticulous practice of the Law of Moses. They also aspired moreover to play a political role. Insofar as Jesus spoke about a major shift in the relationship between Israel and God and announced that God was concerned with the whole world and not only the chosen people, the Pharisees felt obliged to oppose him in the name of the integrity of Judaism.

In all religious controversies between the Jews, hard words and fearsome denunciations rained down: we need only to peruse the Old Testament prophets. So if Jesus sometimes vilified the Pharisees, if he attacked them openly (or more covertly in certain parables), he also had more peaceful debates with them. He even had friends among them, since some were trying to evolve and adapt their rites and rules to a changing society, to the point that the intransigent Essenians accused them of backsliding.

Finally, one significant point should be emphasized: Pharisees do not appear among his accusers in any of the accounts of the Passion of Jesus. On the contrary, some actually warned him of the danger he was running.

Mary Magdalene

At the time of Jesus, Judaism was not the only religion to believe in the existence of demons that could possess people and which could be driven out with suitable prayers or rites. And since medical knowledge was not very advanced, psychoses and phenomena such as epilepsy were often ascribed to demonic "possession." Jesus, however, did agree (occasionally with reservations) to free those he met of diseases or other physical and mental ailments that tormented them. In this way, he practiced exorcism. The most famous of those on whom he performed is Mary Magdalene, although her exorcism is alluded to and mentioned only in a single Gospel (Luke 8:2).

Mary was of Magdala, the Aramaic name for a sizable town located on the banks of the Lake of Tiberias. Wrongly, she has been regarded as a prostitute. This is because Magdala, at the time of the revolt against the Romans in 66, was sacked by the latter, an occurrence the rabbis interpreted as divine punishment for the "depravity" of its inhabitants. Hence the notion that Mary Magdalene, who had lived there, must have possessed loose morals. It is also thought that she may have been wealthy since she belonged to the group of women who followed Jesus and his companions and assisted them with their "resources." During the reign of Herod Antipas, there was something of a boom in the Magdala region.

The Evangelists put particular stress on the fact that Mary Magdalene accompanied Jesus right up to his death, whereas the proper disciples (proper) had fled. She helped to embalm his body and, shortly after the Sabbath, was the first to discover the empty tomb. Finally, according to the Gospel of John, Jesus, having appeared to her, chose her to inform his companions of the news. This is why in the Middle Ages she was called the apostle of the apostles, "apostola apostolorum." It is this closeness to Jesus that has given rise to so many legends.

DANGER
APPROACHES

Rejoice heart and soul, daughter of Zion!
Shout for joy, daughter of Jerusalem!
Look, your King is approaching, he is vindicated
and victorious, humble and riding on a donkey,
on a colt, the foal of a donkey. He will
banish chariots from Ephraim, and
horses from Jerusalem; the bow of war
will be banished. He will proclaim
peace to the nations
(Zech. 9:9—10).

But Jesus said:"Let the little children alone, and do not stop them from coming to me;
for it is to such as these that the kingdom of heaven belongs"

(Matt. 19:14).

THE RETURN TO JERUSALEM

•:·················:•

Jesus knew only too well: to go to Jerusalem was to put his life in the balance. But Jerusalem was the heartbeat of Israel and it was there that his message, sooner or later, had to be spread. There, in and around the Temple, thousands of pilgrims were attracted from Judea, Galilee, and from all the shores of the Mediterranean where Jewish people had been living for centuries.

These pilgrims were the lifeblood of the city, buying curios and fabrics, and most especially animals that were offered as sacrifices at the Temple. And they also paid fees to the priests. At certain periods there was even a regulation stipulating that pious Jews on pilgrimage must spend a tenth of their annual income in the capital city.

The Temple was the largest employer in the city, with a staff of hundreds, including guards and Levites (a kind of second-category clergy, responsible for policing the Temple, preparing sacrifices, exacting taxes, and so on). And all of those who did not actually work for the Temple, the craftsmen in the lower city—potters, weavers, stonemasons—survived only by dint

of serving the high priests, the sacerdotal caste, and the notables of the upper city about whom they had hardly a good word to say. The social situation was then often tense. But Jerusalem would rally round the Temple, since, among the most devout, the Temple was the only reason for living and afforded a livelihood for all the others.

According to the Gospel of John (the others are less clear), Jesus traveled to Jerusalem on five occasions. The most significant trip was about six months before the Passover, which was to mark his death, for the festival of the Tents (or feast of Shelters), one of the three great feasts to which pilgrims would flock. By the time he arrived it was drawing to a close, but he started speaking to the droves of people in the Temple. His words caused such uproar that some wanted to lynch him there and then (John 7:1–34).

Jesus could have then easily predicted that his reappearance in Jerusalem would be met with relentless hostility. But Christ said with bitter irony, "it would not be right for a prophet to die outside Jerusalem" (Luke 13:33). It's not that he wanted

As they persisted with their question he straightened up and said,
"Let the one among you who is guiltless be the first to throw a stone at her"

(John 8:7).

to die, but he knew that his mission—to tell people who God really was—would upset the powers that be so much that they would do all they could to silence him. As he preached, the threats became more numerous.

One day, having lunched at a Pharisee's home without performing ablutions prior to the meal (the purification of the body with water as prescribed by custom), an argument burst out. And Jesus said to some "lawyers" (interpreters of the Law) present: "You load on people burdens that are unendurable, burdens you yourselves do not touch with your fingertips" (Luke 11:46). When he had left, they "tried to force answers from him . . . lying in wait to catch him out in something he might say" (Luke 11:53–54).

A little later, according to the same Evangelist, when Jesus was traveling to Jerusalem, some Pharisees approached and informed him: "Go away," they said, "leave this place because Herod means to kill you" (Luke 13:31). Perhaps they harbored good intentions, but maybe too they would have liked to be rid of him.

His companions could not believe that the risk he was running was real. In their eyes, he was the Messiah, and thus invincible. Seeing that the crowds hailing and listening to him were dwindling, however, they at last took fright. "They were on the road, going up to Jerusalem; Jesus was walking on ahead of them; they were in a daze; and those who followed were apprehensive" (Mark 10:32).

How could a man, traveling from village to village and from town to town, repeating in every way he knew the same message of boundless love, become the target of such threats? There are a number of possible answers to this quandary.

The first relates to Jesus' attitude with regard to the Law of Moses. He affirmed without hesitation that he did not come to abolish or "destroy" the Law, "but to complete" it (Matt. 5:17). But, while he did complete it, he also went beyond it, like a fruit goes beyond a seed, sometimes killing it. And even if Jesus often acted like a good Jew, quoted the Scriptures, and observed the majority of Jewish customs (while admittedly being rather free with the Sabbath when need be), he spoke a new language.

In the very famous Sermon on the Mount, in particular, Jesus proclaimed: "You have heard how it was said, You will love your neighbor, and hate your enemy. But I say this to you, love your enemies and pray for those who persecute you" (Matt. 5:43–44). He repeated this phrase on no less than five occasions. Thus he opposed his own authority to that of the Law and the prophets.

However, the great Moses himself had not claimed to be the author of the Law: it had been transmitted to him by God. And the prophets did not say they were the sources of their insights. When they pronounced rules or denounced abuses, they never failed to add: "Thus spoke Yahweh." Jesus spoke and spoke in his own name.

Even more than this: he pardoned sins, which is a prerogative of God alone. No prophet would have permitted himself such a liberty. Jesus pardoned the sins of a woman who wiped his feet with her hair during a meal. He asked for no penance. He simply said: "Your faith has saved you; go in peace" (Luke 7:50). It is the faith then that saves, not the penitence, not the sacrifice. But the guests at the meal asked one another: "Who is this man, that even forgives sins?" (Luke 7:49).

*"Master, this woman was caught in the very act of committing adultery,
and in the Law Moses has ordered us to stone women of this kind.
What have you got to say?"*

(John 8:4–5).

He thus arrogated powers reserved for God. He himself said that he was imparting a new message from God to humankind: "My teaching is not from myself, it comes from the one that sent me" (John 7:16). Then he went even further, saying that he was "at one with the Father," and thus that he participated in the divine.

In an epoch-making event for all humanity, it was a fundamentally new image of God that emerged. But, at the time, it was the theocratic powers of the Temple, founded on the old image, which appeared threatened.

This his companions realized, but they reckoned that one day or another Jesus would foment an uprising and carry all before him. Such, as can be deduced from a reading of the Gospels, were the thoughts that agitated them as they approached Jerusalem a few days before the great festival of Pesach that commemorates the passage of the Jews out of Egypt and is also the feast of unleavened bread (unleavened because the escapees were in such a hurry to leave the country of Pharaoh that they had no time to let the dough rise).

Nearing Jerusalem, according to Matthew, Mark, and Luke, Jesus sent two emissaries out before him: "Go to the village facing you and you will at once find a tethered donkey and a colt with her. Untie them and bring them to me. If anyone says anything to you, you are to say, 'The Master needs them'"(Matt 21:2–3). Why did Christ want to enter to Jerusalem mounted on an ass (or donkey)? Matthew recalls an Old Testament prophecy that tells the "daughter of Zion: Look, your king is approaching, humble and riding on a donkey" (Matt. 21:5). And according to the prophet Zechariah this king who is "humble and riding on a donkey," who will "banish . . . horses from Jerusalem; and the bow of battle will be banished" [violence rendered useless], and "he will proclaim peace to the nations [to the heathen too]" (Zech. 9:9–10). So which "heathens" did the Jews loathe the most? The Romans, of course.

Jesus then, if one accepts the interpretation provided by Matthew, wanted to make his entrance into Jerusalem as a messenger of peace. There, he was hailed not by a serried crowd, but by the odd huddle. Yet the lanes were narrow, so the smallest gathering could feel like a mob. Jesus stood at the head of a few groups of pilgrims, probably the majority from Galilee, those who remained faithful to him. There they chanted and prayed. Nothing much there to worry a Roman garrison, which was reinforced at Passover time to forestall incidents. So it did not intervene. But the arrival of Jesus, even alone, would have been enough to disturb the men of the Temple who were ever on the lookout for any pretext to have him condemned—as the story of the woman taken in adultery shows: "In the Law Moses has ordered us to stone women of this kind. What have you to say?" (John 8:5). But Jesus preached leniency and had not come to apply the Law of Moses. The ultimate ordeal was getting closer.

Then he went into the Temple and began driving out those who were busy trading, saying to them,
"According to scripture, My house shall be a house of prayer, but you have turned it into a bandits' den"
(Luke 19:45–46).

THE MERCHANTS IN THE TEMPLE

One of the most striking scenes of the Gospel, the one in which Jesus drove the merchants from the Temple, is often misconstrued or regarded as little more than an anecdote. It was this act, however, that precipitated Jesus' arrest—as he must have realized. But even more than this, it illuminates the very nature of God.

The story is well known. The pilgrims would assemble in the Temple to sacrifice their animals. An end of human sacrifice had been instituted when Abraham, about to cut the throat of his own son, had his hand stayed by Jehovah and replaced Isaac with a ram. It was this substitution that became the rule. The Jews coming to the Temple would offer as sacrifices animals without defects, lambs or doves in particular, or sometimes, for the wealthier, oxen. These they would buy in the Temple enclosure, thereby guaranteeing the purity of the victims.

They would also buy them using money from the Temple: on entering, they would change the impure money they had brought from outside—all the more contaminated since,

coming from various regions, some of the currencies would perhaps have been minted with religious symbols anathema to the faithful of Jehovah. It must be stressed that these were all normal activities, essential to the smooth running of the Temple. If the moneychangers and animal dealers had not been there, then sacrifice would have been simply impossible. As the Jewish historian Flavius Josephus wrote, however: "No Jew could seriously think of abandoning [the sacrifices] and would be more ready to lose his life than forsake the divine cult he has been ordered to render to God."

Mixing with the heaving crowd around the stalls of the money-changers and those selling beasts destined to die, Jesus, without a moment's thought, seized a whip, and drove them out together with their animals, upending tables and scattering the money on the ground, as John relates. The mob, the screams and rising dust, the lowing of the cattle and the cackling of the doves can only be imagined. This is the only scene in the Gospel in which Jesus manifests any violence whatsoever.

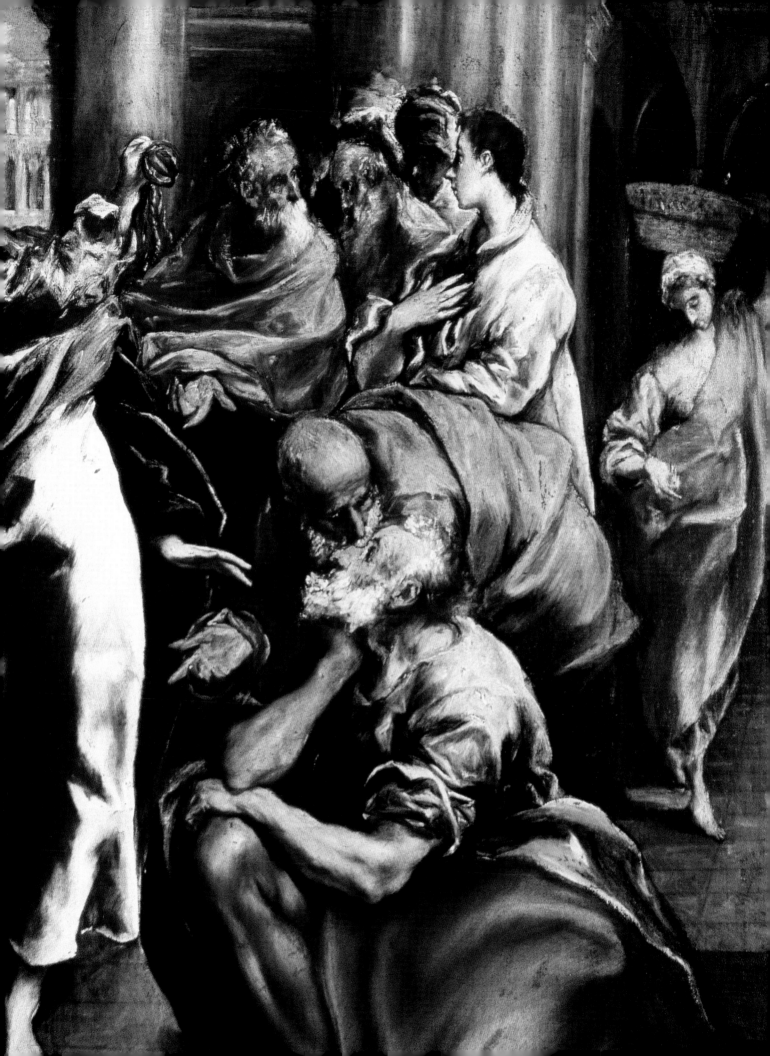

One mistake in interpretation is often made in connection with this event. Many compare these merchants to sellers of pious objects such as statuettes or souvenir pictures still found today around pilgrimage sites. But Jesus was not concerned here with such sidelines. Animal sacrifice, as Flavius Josephus underlined, lay at the heart of Jewish piety and was the central activity at the Temple: it was this Christ denounced.

He even explained why, armed with a "whip out of cords," he beat sellers and buyers alike: "Stop using my Father's house as a market" (John 2:16). This doesn't mean Christ condemned trade, exchange, and barter as a whole: the money was on the side, to pay for merchandise or services rendered by third parties. What Jesus meant was that there was to be no such trading with God. Commerce is a give-and-take process: I give you this and, in return, you give me that. With God, there should be no such give-and-take. With Him there is, as it were, "give" and no "take." An absolute, free, and perfect gift.

God did not ask for sacrifice—and even less did he want the sacrifice of his Son to take away the sins of the world—as is often alleged. Josef Ratzinger, now Pope Benedict XVI, wrote: "Certain devotional texts seem to suggest that the Christian faith in the Cross represents a God whose inexorable justice demanded a human sacrifice, the sacrifice of his own Son. Widespread though this image may be, it is quite false."

Sacrifice can then be interpreted in two ways. First, as a currency used in trading with the divine. Second, as the highest expression of the gift of self to others: a mother who throws herself in the flames to save her child, for example. The first type of sacrifice—used to "pay off" the divinity—has been practiced by most civilizations: by the Jewish people, but also by the Egyptians, the Aztecs of South America and others.

It is then quite understandable that Jesus' disciples, when it came to interpreting his death on the Cross—such an extraordinary and painful surprise for them, since the Messiah expected by the Jews was meant to reign over all—saw it, mistakenly, as a sacrifice of this nature. If Jesus died, it was not so that his Father might forgive humanity. It was because he embraced the risks of his mission and these risks included his death. This then is the second form of sacrifice.

He knew very well that, in chasing the merchants from the Temple, he was exposing himself to danger. These merchants were no tradesmen, but in general priests or Levites, men in the service of the Temple who obeyed the caste of the high priests and the Sadducees. They were already terribly wary of Jesus, since his sayings and acts were occasionally at variance with the Law and he was not above criticizing their office. But this time, on two grounds, he had gone still further.

First of all, he attacked them financially, since patently all this activity turned a healthy profit. And, more indirectly, he also undermined all those who, in Jerusalem, lived from pilgrimages—that is to say, from "religious tourism."

The second reason was still more crucial: to attack the Temple, not only verbally but physically, was to attack the very symbol of the presence of God in Israel, the protection afforded by God to His people. This was unacceptable not only to the Sadducees but also to every inhabitant of Jerusalem.

The Romans must have been perturbed at all the fuss Jesus was stirring up. The key point in their eyes was to preserve law and order. Jesus could hardly have counted for much: he was but another self-proclaimed prophet. The high priests could get rid of Christ just by delivering him up to them. In this way, they could also earn points for good conduct as was cynically expressed by the high priest, Caiaphas: "You fail to see that it is to your advantage that one man should die for the people rather than the whole nation should perish" (John 11:50). Obviously, Jesus was not unaware of all these pitfalls. So if he struck at the Temple, it was because to him the act was so crucial that he was prepared to come face to face with death.

TINTORETTO. *THE LAST SUPPER.* 1578–81.
SCUOLA GRANDE DI SAN ROCCO. VENICE.

THE LAST SUPPER

·:·················:·

Another feast-day—but this would be the last and they all knew it. Since their arrival in Jerusalem, the companions of Jesus had scurried through its streets and lanes; alarmed, they keep on the move, ever watchful, eyes peeled, ready to unmask spies, flush out informers, protect the Master, this man for whom they have given up and risked their all. And there they were, that very evening, gathered together, still anxious, but somehow relieved.

The Jewish people enjoyed feasting and conviviality. A meal allowed them to come together and share in the sight of Jehovah. Many tales in the Old Testament begin or end with eating in company, as do many episodes in the Gospel. This particular meal was lit by the light of the most beautiful festival of all, Passover. The meal at Passover, the Seder, marked an essential time of year for the disciples.

They had never before gathered in the large room, which a friend of theirs had found for them. They must have arrived stealthily. From the Mount of Olives where they had set up camp, Jesus sent Peter and John in the vanguard. At the entrance to the city, they were to meet a man carrying a pitcher of water and "follow him into the house he enters" (Luke 22:10).

The apostles and Jesus reposed on benches as custom demanded, showing how, since departing from Egypt, the chosen people were free.

John the Evangelist (and he alone) described a scene, which left the apostles flabbergasted. In the middle of the meal Jesus stood up, left his place presiding over the table, disrobed, and girded a strip of linen like a loincloth—just as his people had done when they were set to work as slaves in Egypt. Then he started to wash the feet of his companions.

Washing feet was not an exceptional rite. Priests, the only ones with the right to penetrate into the Temple, had to do so since they walked through it barefoot. Thus, since their religion called for great care of feet, basins intended for such ablutions were found at the entrance to their residences. Neither was the act of washing feet their exclusive prerogative: it was practiced throughout the Middle East to honor a guest. But usually, it was

He came to Simon Peter, who said to him, "Lord, are you going to wash my feet?" Jesus answered,
"At the moment, you do not know what I am doing, but later you will understand"

(John 13:6–7).

entrusted to an inferior, to a servant. To wash someone's feet was tantamount to recognizing one's inferiority: the wife did so for her husband, while children cleansed the feet of their father. Although most often it was the task of servants.

It is then hardly surprising that Peter, who was never one to hold back and is often presented in the Gospels as the spokesman for the group, started to protest: "'Lord, are you going to wash my feet?'" And Jesus replied: "At the moment, you do not know what I am doing, but later you will understand." This answer however did not satisfy the apostle: "You shall never wash my feet" (John 13:6–8).

Jesus then provided two answers, two explanations. The first to Peter alone: "If I do not wash you, you can have no share with me" (John 13:8). In other words: they would be separate—no longer in the same camp. The point then was extremely important. He addressed his second response to all. After regaining his place, his task finished, he said: "You call me Master and Lord, and rightly: so I am. If I, then, your Master and Lord, have washed your feet you must wash each other's feet." (John 13:13–14). Thus Jesus, who could no longer be in any doubt as to his fate, laid down the rules of the little community that had to survive him: each of his companions had to live as servant to the group.

The scene has still another, highly significant meaning. Jesus, God-Man, Man-God, knelt at the feet of men to show what God really was: humble, a servant; the opposite of the all-powerful monarch such as usually pictured. This meant that spiritual power consisted in bowing freely before the lowliest.

On the spur of the moment, the apostles were probably unable to grasp the meaning of this scene, because it was quickly followed by the drama of the break with Judas. He had hardly put his clothes back on when Jesus announced: "One of you is going to betray me" (John 13:21). This did not appear to surprise them overmuch; they lived in such fear that they had lost all self-assurance. "The disciples looked at each other, wondering whom he meant" (John 13:22). You could have cut the atmosphere with a knife. Peter could not bear it and made a sign to the disciple seated in the best position to question Jesus since he was on his right. Jesus answered: "It is the one to whom I give the piece of bread that I dip in the dish" (John 13:26). But this act normally is meant to honor the recipient. What could Jesus possibly have meant?

He addressed Judas: "What you are going to do, do quickly" (John 13:27). Why did he encourage Judas to leave? And what did he know of his intentions? These questions have given rise to divergent interpretations. Rather implausibly, John the Evangelist implies that the apostles thought Jesus sent Judas out to buy food or offer alms to the poor.

Then began the third act of this exceptional meal: the sharing of the bread and the wine, the institution that Christians call the Eucharist or Holy Communion. Oddly, John the Evangelist passed over it in silence. Although he was the only one to record Jesus' remark after the miracle of the loaves and fishes: "Whoever eats my flesh and drinks my blood lives in me and I live in that person" (John 6:56).

With or without Judas (according to Luke he was still present), as the meal came to an end, Jesus took the bread, prayed, broke it, and handed it to the apostles. "This," he said "is my body given for you." He then did the same thing with the wine cup: "This cup is the new covenant in my blood poured out for you" (Luke 22:17–20).

The extreme brevity of the account from which the Roman Catholic Church was to draw such an essential sacrament should be noted. There were just a few lines without further comment in Matthew, Mark, and Luke. The apostle Paul was more forthcoming. In the First Epistle to the

Then taking a cup he gave thanks and said, "Take this and share it among you, because from now on,
I tell you, I shall never again drink wine until the kingdom of God comes"
(Luke 22:17–18).

Corinthians—whom he had evangelized and who were wandering from the straight and narrow—after giving them a piece of his mind, Paul returned to the account of the Last Supper and offered a version that corresponded to those of Matthew and Luke, but added, twice, Christ's instruction: "Do this in memory of me" (1 Cor. 11:24).

Jesus' mention of the "covenant" (or "testament") should also be underlined. The theme of testament or covenant recurs in the Bible. Jehovah entered into various covenants with men. Initially he did so with humanity as a whole through Noah, by way of rules: do not kill—respect one another. Then with the Jewish people through the covenant with Abraham and another rule: obey God and your conscience. Next on Mount Sinai with Moses, to whom God presented, in awesome detail, the Law.

Finally through Jesus, the covenant became even tighter. Since Jesus was God incarnate, made flesh, it meant that God and humanity were indissolubly linked. This "covenant" was "eternal," Jesus said, because men, would never be able to break it. They would not be able to change the fact that Christ was at once man and God. And the covenant was forged so as to pursue its creation, a task common to God and humanity.

All this, of course, would have hardly occurred to the apostles on the evening of the Last Supper. They lived in the present moment. They heard Jesus announce his departure in tender terms: "Little children, I shall be with you only a little longer" (John 13:33). And when Peter grew troubled: "Lord, where are you going?... Why cannot I not follow you now? I will lay down my life for you," he received the well-known reply: "In all truth, I tell you, before the cock crows you will have disowned me three times" (John 13:36–38). Jesus, however, went on to reassure them: "Do not let your hearts be troubled.... In my Father's house there are many places to live in" (John, 14, 1–2), before finally breaking up the company— he was going to his death and his companions would sleep. It was, in all probability, April 7, 30 CE.

PRECEDING PAGE

LEONARDO DA VINCI, *THE LAST SUPPER*, 1495–97.
REFECTORY, SANTA MARIA DELLA GRAZIE, MILAN.

BELOW

DOMENICO GHIRLANDAIO, *THE LAST SUPPER*, 1481.
OGNISSANTI, FLORENCE.

Judea and the Romans

Palestine had been absorbed into the Roman Empire in 63 BCE. The new masters had applied various policies, hesitating between direct rule and government through local authorities, the king, or high priest.

Herod the Great, who died in 4 BCE, had eclipsed the high priest. His son, Antipas, as a Galilean, showed himself a skillful politician, forestalling serious disorder. The Romans thus kept him in power until, in the year 39, he was misguided enough to ask to Emperor Caligula to crown him king, whereas he was only a tetrarch.

It was soon clear that another son of Herod, Archelaos, was not up to the task in Judea. The Romans thus placed a prefect at the head of both the administration and the local legions, dependent in his turn on a "legate" based in Syria and especially on the legions the latter could send him as reinforcements in the event of insurrection. Ensconced at Caesarea on the coast, the prefect was seldom resident in Jerusalem, and thus relied on the high priests.

By and large, the Romans were respectful of the religious rites of their subject peoples. Legionaries profaning or carrying out acts offensive to Judaism were transferred or even put to death. Roman legions in maneuvers steered clear of Judea so as not to have to raise their standard bearing the portrait of the emperor. The Romans knew by bitter experience that the Jews would not tolerate the practice since he was considered to be a god. Though disdaining them, they thus respected the customs of the Jews. In their eyes, they were atheists. In the next century, the Roman historian Tacitus dubbed them an "abominable race."

In Jerusalem, at the time of major pilgrimages, the Romans would remain on high alert, and reinforce the garrison situated in a tower called Antonia. They cordoned off the town with soldiers who inspected the crowd. In the ordinary course of events, these legionaries, recruited from every territory Rome had conquered, would keep out of sight.

PAOLO VERONESE. *THE CENTURION AT CAPERNAUM ASKING JESUS TO CURE HIS PARALYZED SERVANT.* 1580. KUNSTHISTORISCHES MUSEUM. VIENNA.

Passover and the Lamb

Passover, which lasted for eight days, was the most important of Jewish feast days. It commemorated their ancestors' departure from Egypt through the Sea of Reeds, today known as the Red Sea. At that time, in principle every Jewish adult would to go to Jerusalem for the celebrations.

Passover began the day before the full moon following the vernal equinox. The paschal meal, of considerable importance, was composed primarily of lamb. God had asked Moses, before leaving Egypt, to have each family slaughter a lamb and smear the blood of the animal on the door of every house to protect the occupiers. Then the lamb—whose bones were not to be broken—was to be consumed by the whole family. Recalled in the book of Exodus (12:11–14), God's orders to Moses were followed year after year by each family—including the mark of blood on the door of the house. The Paschal Lamb was to be eaten entire and its remains burnt before sunrise.

After his death and Resurrection, Jesus' contemporaries saw him as the Paschal Lamb that saved man at the expense of his own blood. They also referred to a text of the prophet Isaiah that spoke of a servant of God: "Ill-treated and afflicted, he never opened his mouth, like a lamb led to the slaughter-house" (Is. 53:7).

According to the Gospel of John, when Jesus came to be baptized by John the Baptist, the latter called him "the Lamb of God that takes away the sin of the world" (John 1:29). Christ was then opposed to evil and to violence, a symbol of gentleness. The same Gospel—in the version that has come down to us dating from the very end of the first century—stresses that the Romans, contrary to custom, did not break the bones of Jesus' legs when he was crucified, thereby reinforcing the allusion to the Paschal Lamb.

In the Apocalypse (or Revelation), Christ is presented as a lamb (or a small ram, depending on the translations), flayed, but alive and raised to glory.

The High Priests

The role of the high priest at that time was primordial. Only the presiding high priest had the right to enter the inner sanctum of the Temple, the Holy of Holies, a place in which God was mysteriously present yet simultaneously absent (for he cannot be enclosed). The high priest also exerted political power: he was authorized by the Romans to administer much everyday business in Jerusalem and in Judea, as long as he could guarantee the payment of taxes and the respect of law and order. He was assisted by a sacerdotal aristocracy (especially his own family) and by lay worthies. The mere priests—whose numbers ran into thousands—took turns to serve in the Temple, but they lived all over the country.

At the time of Jesus, high priests were selected among the Sadducees, a politico-religious group, which seemed to come to prominence from only around the second century BCE. Not all Sadducees belonged to the "clergy." They constituted a kind of aristocracy or noble class, often wrestling for power with the Pharisees, for they were liable at any time to lose it, as would happen during the reign of Herod the Great.

Their religious ideas are poorly understood. They were opposed to Jesus in a controversy concerning the resurrection of the dead, in which they did not believe. According to the Jewish historian Flavius Josephus, they did not expect the advent of the Messiah. They preached that it was necessary to observe the Law to the letter, in an almost legalistic manner, and on this point they were on a collision course with Jesus.

The Sadducees, however, collaborated readily with the Roman occupants, who permitted the exercise of this otherwise relatively conservative religion. They were also influenced by Greek culture and some had adopted Grecian ways. Not without reason, the general population, on whom they looked down, regarded them as opportunists, while respecting the high priest for the function he discharged.

Unquestionably though, the Sadducees were determined to safeguard the nation. At the time of Jesus, the high priest was Caiaphas, who held the post between 18 and 36 CE. The Sadducees would fall from grace when the Temple was destroyed by the Romans in 70 CE. The Pharisees, who "controlled" the synagogues, then began to exert their hegemony.

THE PASSION

Like a sapling he grew up before him, like a root in arid ground. He had no form or charm to attract us, no beauty to win our hearts; he was despised, the lowest of man, a man of sorrows, familiar with suffering, one from whom as it were we averted our gaze, despised for whom we had no regard. Yet ours were the sufferings he was bearing, ours the sorrows he was carrying, while we thought of him as someone being punished and struck with affliction by God; whereas he was being wounded for our rebellions (Isa. 53:2—5).

Then Jesus said to them, "You will all fall away from me tonight, for the scripture says, 'I shall strike the shepherd and the sheep of the flock will be scattered,' but after my resurrection I shall go ahead of you to Galilee"

(Matt. 26:31–32).

GETHSEMANE

•:·················:•

Then came the final ordeal. Jesus and his followers had sung the Hallel, the thanksgiving that concluded the Last Supper. Then they departed, crossing the lower districts of Jerusalem to Cedron, a brook which, in spring, flowed with foul, muddy water. It was the time of the full moon; the scene was bathed in pallid light. Jesus often went to a place on the Mount of Olives called *Gethsemane* in Greek, in Aramaic Hebrew *Gat-semani*, which means "oil-press."

The apostles were listless, overwhelmed, yet moved by the episodes they had just witnessed. Apparently, not a word was exchanged throughout the journey. But in this large garden, Jesus asked some of them to rest—according to some traditions—in a kind of cave, saying "Stay here while I pray" (Mark 14:32). He continued on the path together with Peter, James, and John, and then halted again: "My soul is sorrowful to the point of death. Wait here and stay awake" (Mark 14:34).

How could Jesus, the very epitome of joy, be sad? And sad "to the point of death"? The expression had already occurred in the Bible, in particular in the mouth of Jonah when he was miserable and "I might as well be dead" (Jonah 4:8). For many theologians referring to the texts of Mark and Matthew, if Jesus spoke like the forlorn prophet, it was partly because he could foresee that his disciples and friends were going to be distraught at his arrest and death and would, having betrayed and disavowed him, be scattered.

After these words, Jesus moved a little farther off. To seek solitude to pray and come into contact with God is a frequent action in the Bible. According to Mark Jesus moved away: "'Abba, Father!' he said, 'For you everything is possible. Take this cup away from me'"(Mark 14:36). In several biblical texts, a chalice or cup stands for the destiny man receives from God.

Soon, however, Jesus accepted his fate: "But let it be as you, not I, would have it" (Mark 14:36). These two sentences, one of refusal and the other of acceptance, obviously voice a confrontation. Up to that point, Jesus had always been in total

Then an angel appeared to him, coming from heaven to give him strength.
In his anguish he prayed even more earnestly and his sweat fell to the ground like great drops of blood
(Luke 22:43–44).

agreement with God, speaking on his behalf, ending up by claiming to be his Son, and asserting that whoever saw him also saw the Father. But here there is, if not opposition, since he expressed total confidence ("For you everything is possible"), but a questioning, a debate, an inner struggle: "anguish" means "struggle." This excludes the idea that Jesus was made incarnate to march blithely to his death from the very beginning. He took a risk and embraced it as the price of his mission, which, as he would soon repeat to Pilate, was to tell the truth, the truth about God.

In the eyes of men, his task was to end in failure. The crowds turned away from him the minute he tried to tell them the most important thing; they wanted only miracles, magic, demonstrations of power, the triumphant march of a king able to drive out the Romans and bring the high priests to heel. This is what the apostles thought too, and especially, perhaps, Judas. At this point, Jesus sensed, or knew, that they would try to condemn him for political or religious ideas that were not his. This is why, according to the Gospels, he would fight so his death preserved its true meaning.

There, however, in a garden planted with olive trees around a press, he was not sure he could do it, not certain he could explain everything, get his point across. He might have even been worried about a summary execution, with no trial, no chance to put his case. So overcome was he that, according to Luke, "his sweat fell to the ground like great drops of blood" (Luke 22:44). A symptom of extreme stress, this very rare phenomenon is known by the name of hemathidrosis, during which subcutaneous blood vessels protrude into the sweat-producing glands, the blood curdles, and the perspiration transports it to the surface of the skin.

Jesus had recovered from the attack when, for the third time, he woke up his companions and told them to get up, his betrayer was not far away. And at once Judas appeared, according to Luke, accompanied by a small troop armed with swords and clubs, coming on behalf of the "chief priests, and captains of the Temple guard, and elders" (Luke 22:52; similar terms were used by Mark and Matthew). Only John added the Pharisees, who were not mentioned again thereafter. Thus Judas, as the account of the Last Supper implied, delivered Jesus to the high priests—in theory for thirty pieces of silver. Matthew paused in his narrative of the Passion to note that afterwards the desperate Judas hanged himself from a tree.

Jesus' companions, now wide awake, began to put up a fight, but Jesus quickly quelled these intimations of resistance. He had no need of this paltry army. He did not want to start a riot, because he has no wish to seize power—above all not through violence. Only Matthew quotes Jesus' famous words: "For all who draw the sword will die by the sword"(Matt. 26:52). An equivalent of this phrase is to be found in the biblical text of Genesis: "He who sheds the blood of man, by man shall his blood be shed" (Gen. 9:6). It was to reappear in certain apocryphal texts. It seems to have been a popular axiom in the Jewish world, inspired by the *lex talionis*, according to which one inflicts on the culprit a punishment comparable in nature to the offence committed.

In fact, one of the disciples (Peter, according to John, who always stressed his fiery character) had already unsheathed his weapon and cut off the ear (the four Gospels are in agreement on this point) of a servant of the high priest called Malchus, a rather common name. This individual poses quite

And at once the cock crowed for the second time, and Peter recalled what Jesus had said to him,
"Before the cock crows twice, you will have disowned me three times"
(Mark 14:72).

a problem for scholars: was he the head of the Temple guards, chief assistant to the high priest, or some other of his henchmen?

One thing seems certain: readers of Gospel, at the end of the first century, saw him as someone who embodied hostility towards Jesus. And if they might naturally have delighted in the misfortunes of their adversaries, Jesus' warning was there to upbraid them: "For all who draw the sword will die by the sword." It was after this admonition, precisely, that the disciples began to abandon their master. Not only through fear, not only because they thought that their little organization was about to fall apart, but because they now understood that he had no intention of seizing power by force.

For up to that point, they had been the victims of a misunderstanding: they had awaited divine intervention on Jesus' behalf—or perhaps they believed that Christ would take matters into his own hands. This was perhaps even what Judas was trying to provoke. But nothing like that was to take place. And so they fled. Another, unnamed individual did likewise. According to Mark: "And a young man followed with nothing on but a linen cloth. They caught hold of him, but he left the cloth in their hands and ran away naked" (Mark 14:51–52). The episode is puzzling. What can it mean?

Initially, the attempt on the part of the unknown youth showed his desire to be faithful to Jesus and not to flee like the others. But it was a pitiful fiasco: indeed as soon as he was seized, he was in such a hurry to take to his heels that he left his loincloth in the hands of his adversaries, preferring the shame of fleeing stark naked (nakedness is obviously shameful in this case), and in these conditions his escape was even more desperate than that of the apostles.

Perhaps Mark, wanting to underline the drama Jesus' arrest represented for Israel, remembered a sentence in the prophet Amos (eighth century BCE) that predicted dire misfortunes for the Jewish people and concluded these reproaches with the picture of disorderly retreat: "The bravest of warriors will jettison his arms and run away that day" (Amos 2:16).

If this could happen to the greatest heroes, it should not be surprising that it happened to this unknown youth and to the disciples themselves. Maybe Matthew and Luke, who knew at least in part the text of Mark, did not report this episode since they did not want to paint the apostles in too negative a light. For they were men who had abandoned everything for Jesus and had accepted countless sacrifices for his sake.

His trial, which immediately followed his arrest, was yet another drama to endure.

And the high priest said to him,"I put you on oath by the living God to tell us if you are Christ, the Son of God." Jesus answered him,"It is you who say it"

(Matt. 26:63–64)

THE TRIAL

•:················:•

So Jesus was in the clutches of the priesthood. One could almost say of their "clan," since his adversaries took him first not to the official high priest, Caiphas, but to his father-in-law, Annas, an individual that at another time and in another place might have been known as the "Godfather." He had not acted as chief priest for fifteen years, but he still bore the honorary title, like many members of the sacerdotal caste who no longer (or had never) exercised any precise function at the Temple.

By taking him to Annas, Caiaphas and his friends, having already decided that Jesus was to die, showed that they were not going to be hamstrung by rules and regulations. Jesus put his finger on it, asking Annas by what right he interrogated him, adding: "I have spoken openly for all the world to hear; . . . I have said nothing in secret" (John 18:20). Apparently, this was an unseemly way to address an ex-high priest, so an officer of the Temple, outraged, slapped Jesus across the face.

Yet this was only the beginning. Though it was forbidden to strike an accused, it was a rule more often honored in the breach. All the more so since everyone believed Jesus to be already condemned. Peter thought so too, the last of the apostles to have followed Jesus. He snuck into Annas' residence, entering the courtyard thanks, as John makes clear, to "that other disciple who was known to the high priest" (John 18:15). Perhaps this was Nicodemus, a worthy and a Pharisee who, according to various episodes in the Gospel of John, seemed favorable to Jesus.

Peter spent part of the night in the yard, amid the police and various subalterns, before being recognized by a maidservant (probably because of his Galilean accent): after denying all knowledge of Jesus on three occasions, he fled in tears. It is possible that the Evangelists stressed this triple disavowal so as to comfort and reassure the early Christians who in the teeth of persecution had reneged their faith (it should not be forgotten that it was at these people the Gospels were aimed).

The cock crowed. Dawn broke. Jesus was dragged along to Caiaphas. The hour of judgment was nigh. But who was to judge Jesus? Once again it seems that due process was not observed, as Matthew, Mark, and Luke indicate that Christ

Then Herod and his soldiers treated him with contempt and made fun of him;
he put a rich cloak on him and sent him back to Pilate.

(Luke 23:11)

was dispatched to the Sanhedrin. This was a High Court num-
bering seventy-one members (God had ordered Moses to
gather together the seventy-one elders of Israel so that the
prophet would not have to bear the burden of his people
alone). These seventy-one split into three groups: priests, elders, and scribes, or scholars. There were perhaps Pharisees
among the scribes, but the Gospels—which present a dim
view of them up to that point—do not mention them. They
were indeed absent from the trial and the judgment alike. In
any case, many specialists cast doubt over whether the
Sanhedrin held full and regular sessions at this period. And if
the Pharisees had been present, such unbending individuals
would surely have voiced some form of protest.

So Jesus now stood before those who had already decided
his doom. For form's sake they questioned him, summoned
witnesses and ended up unearthing two people willing to
repeat Jesus' remarks concerning the destruction of the
Temple. Christ kept his counsel. On the other hand, when
Caiaphas solemnly asked him whether he was the Son of God,
the Christ, the Son of the "Blessed" (the Gospels use all three
expressions), he answered in the affirmative, adding: "The Son
of Man will be seated at the right hand of the power of God"
(Luke 22:69).

For those present, the expression had a precise meaning:
they believed that one day in the future, Israel would receive
the power from God to judge the nations. Jesus, however, said

the power was for him. For his judges that amounted to a double blasphemy. But they preferred to have a political reason for hauling their prisoner off to the Romans. This too was not hard to find since his answers to their questions could be construed as a claim to be the Messiah, a man intent on grabbing power. And *that* would concern the Romans. Directly.

Why did they have to take Jesus to Pilate? The usual answer is that, since the year 6, the Jewish judges had lost the right to apply the death penalty.

But the Romans did permit them to mete out capital punishment in blatant cases of lawbreaking: for example, if men broke into prohibited areas of the Temple. This remained however very much the exception. Finally, and above all, Caiaphas, who was on good terms with Pilate, probably thought it would be a clever political move to present him with Jesus at the time of the Passover—all the more so since the Roman prefect had taken the precautionary measure (there was always the potential for popular disturbance) of residing in Jerusalem. Caiaphas had already said on an earlier occasion: "It is to your advantage that one man should die for the people, rather than that the whole nation should perish" (John 11:50). He would offer a concession (just as many rulers do when their country is occupied), albeit a dishonorable one. He was intent on saving the body of the nation—even at the price of forfeiting its soul. Moreover, in the immediate future, the risk of the people turning the tables on Caiaphas seemed limited: the affair of the merchants in the Temple had sparked no

riots. Jesus' following among the pilgrims—and even more so among the denizens of Jerusalem—was withering.

Exhausted by hours of interrogation, beatings, and torture, Jesus was dragged off to the Praetorium, or courtroom, the place where Pilate handed down his judgments. His cape fastened at the shoulder, the Roman emerged and lent an ear to the indictment. Since the accusers could not use religious pretexts to condemn Jesus—Pilate did not care about such matters—they accused him instead of claiming to be King of the Jews, adding that he preached revolt and prevented law-abiding citizens from paying their taxes (something very far from the truth).

Plainly the whole sorry tale was of scant interest to Pilate. He asked Jesus what he had done to deserve to be brought to him in this manner. Then Jesus offered the key to his mission: "I came into the world for this, to bear witness to the truth; and all who are on the side of truth listen to my voice" (John 18:37). That is all they got out of him: he has been made incarnate only to say who God truly was.

But Pilate riposted: "What is the truth?" A typically Roman response, since for Romans truth was the real, the material, and Pilate was well acquainted with the Greeks and their eternal discussions on the question. It amounted to saying that, in Pilate's opinion, there was no definitive conclusion on the subject. He was indifferent to the whole business and he ended it by packing off Jesus, a Galilean, to the tetrarch of Galilee, Herod Antipas, who had also made his way to Jerusalem for

TITIANVS ·F

Jesus then came out wearing the crown of thorns and the purple robe.
Pilate said,"Here is the man"

(John 19:5).

"I have sinned. I have betrayed innocent blood." They replied: "What is that to us? That is your concern."
And flinging down the silver in the sanctuary he made off, and went and hanged himself

(Matt. 27: 4–5).

Passover. This was an attractive option, since Pilate didn't like Herod—he would let him deal with this wasp's nest.

Herod Antipas was overjoyed: he has long wanted to meet Jesus. Haunted by the memory of his bloody murder, he even thought Jesus might be the reincarnation of John the Baptist. He questioned the prisoner, who, weary, scornful, did not deign to answer. The envoys from the priest caste were up in arms, so Antipas returned the defendant to Pilate. Jesus was sent from pillar to post, the butt of abuse, the victim of hatred, a pawn in political shenanigans. In ridicule the guards even robed him in a purple (or scarlet) cloak, like a kind of circus king.

So he was back with Pilate who was already holding three Jewish prisoners in chains, including Barabbas, an insurgent arrested after a riot. Custom had it (so the Evangelists inform us though it is recorded nowhere else) that every year at Passover Pilate would grant a pardon to one Jewish prisoner and have him released. Pilate had no pressing desire to have Jesus executed. Matthew moreover recorded (but he was the only one to do so in a few lines of which the historical veracity is a matter of considerable dispute) that, following a dream, Pilate's wife pleaded for Jesus. Pilate then offered the Jews present the right to choose who would be released: Barabbas or the one he derisively dubbed, "the King of the Jews." Urged on by the high priests' clan, those present cried "Barabbas!"

Then, betraying a cruel side, Pilate hesitated not a second longer. When "the chief priests" (alone, according to John) or the crowd they had whipped up (according to the three other Gospels) demanded that Jesus be crucified, he promptly handed him over. The life of this Jew was of no account to him. He was further goaded on by the clans of Annas and Caiaphas who shouted: "If you set him free you are no friend of Caesar's; anyone who makes himself king is defying Caesar" (John 19:12). This was implicit blackmail, because Jews were empowered to appeal to Rome against a prefect or procurator. So Pilate decided to let Jesus die, since they wanted it so much.

Judas for one did acknowledge that he had delivered up an "innocent" and hurried to the high priests to throw the silver he had received back into their faces. Then, according to the Gospel of Matthew (27: 3-10), he hanged himself. Luke, however, the principal author of the Acts of the Apostles, has him perishing by accident in the field bought "with the reward he got for his wickedness" (Acts 1: 18). The two divergent accounts are both inspired by texts from earlier Scriptures: the Evangelists, for whom the crucifixion of Christ was an unbelievable outrage, were concerned to demonstrate to their readers that many aspects of it had been prefigured in the Prophets. The historian meanwhile was less forthcoming.

Large numbers of people followed him, and women too, who mourned and lamented for him.
But Jesus turned to them and said, 'Daughters of Jerusalem, do not weep for me; weep rather for
yourselves and for your children
(Luke 23:28).

PIETER BRUEGHEL THE YOUNGER.
THE CALVARY OF CHRIST, 1607.
JOHNNY VAN HAEFTEN GALLERY, LONDON.

DEATH

He was hauled through narrow alleys bordered by stalls, through lanes teeming with pilgrims and city-dwellers busying themselves with final preparations for the feast day. The rumor spread like wildfire. The Galilean was going to be crucified: the curious and the fanatical, sympathizers and broken-hearted believers alike all flocked to the allotted place. Christ struggled through the mob, staggering under the weight of the beam he carried; as the route twisted and turned, he was besmirched by the sun that dried and burned the blood in his wounds. There were soldiers in front— "Gangway!"—who wielded their sticks every now and again to carve a way through the gawkers. Jesus fell to the ground. Someone would have to help him to carry the great wooden beam to the end. The centurion who was leading the procession, and who would later check that Jesus had expired and certify his death, grabbed a pilgrim, a certain Simon from Cyrene in North Africa (now in Libya), a city which had a large population of Jews.

Romans were fond of getting Jewish pilgrims to perform humiliating tasks—and this was certainly humiliating. The centurion was surely in a hurry to get it all over, to escape from the volatile crowd, and as soon as possible reach Golgotha. This was a rocky outcrop at the gates of Jerusalem to the northwest, called "the field of the skull," covered in gardens and tombs, which the Romans had chosen as their place of execution.

On the stake to which Jesus was to be fixed—as was the rule—Pilate had stuck a piece of wood bearing the reason for the victim's condemnation. Mockingly, it read: "Jesus of Nazareth, King of the Jews"; in Latin: "*Iesu Nazareticu Rex Judeorum*" or INRI. Apparently the high priests protested, but Pilate ignored them.

Jesus arrived at Golgotha, his strength failing rapidly. He was yanked, dragged —"carried" according to Mark. The soldiers stripped him. It was a Roman custom designed to debase the victim still further. His paltry possessions were handed to the executioners as a bonus. This too was the custom.

They enlisted a passer-by, Simon of Cyrene, father of Alexander and Rufus,
who was coming in from the country, to carry his cross
(Mark 15:21).

Then they crucified him. The Evangelists provide neither details nor precise indications. As if their outrage at this torment, their pain and anger had stayed their hand. According to Mark, Luke, and Matthew, two "criminals" or "thieves" (in John they were two unknown men) were crucified with him. One of them found the strength to insult Jesus, joining his voice to that of a motley crowd made up of the curious and merciless adversaries, of pilgrims arriving in Jerusalem and a handful of the faithful. Mostly women. No text quotes a single apostle.

John, however, refers to the presence of the "disciple whom [Jesus] loved" and of Mary, his mother (John 19:26). The figures at the foot of the cross were ignored by the three Evangelists. In fact, under various emperors of the time, the families of condemned men were forbidden to approach the body of the victim. John is the only one to recount the scene in which Jesus entrusted his "mother" (who is not called by her name) to the "disciple whom Jesus loved," who was to take "her into his home" (John 19:27).

The majority of specialists do not regard this as historical fact. As they see it, when the dying Jesus called on the "woman," he meant Israel—the Israel, which awaited salvation from God. The disciple has been afforded the revelation of what God is. The point was to symbolize the shift from the old to the new dispensation.

Furthermore, the disciple did not need to lodge Mary. The Acts of the Apostles (written in the main by Luke) recount that after the Ascension they "were joined constantly in prayer together with some women, including Mary the mother of Jesus, and with his brothers" (Acts 1:14).

The same Luke, in his account of the Crucifixion, emphasizes that the third crucified man rallied to Jesus and recognized him for what he was. The episode, though disputed, is pregnant with hope. Luke presents the Passion as a battle during which Jesus had already landed his blows, and from which, in the final analysis, he emerged victorious.

It is at this juncture, however, that the insults born of hatred on the one side and of disappointment on the other grew still harsher. There came the same challenge the devil had issued in the wilderness: since you are so powerful, show it by extricating yourself and calling on your angels for assistance.

As for the Roman legionaries, they displayed a measure of indulgence. They disposed of an old recipe that could quell a burning thirst and allay heatstroke: *posca*, water soured with vinegar. One of them soaked a sponge in it, stuck it on a reed, and lifted it to the parched lips of the bloodstained martyr. The sun was at its zenith. Jesus cried out in Aramaic: "*Eloi, Eloi, lama sabachtani?*" meaning: "My God, my God, why have you forsaken me?" The plea comes from verse 1 of Psalm 22, which ends by praising God for answering the supplication: "For he has not despised nor disregarded the poverty of the poor, has not turned his face away, but has listened to the cry for help."

The afternoon drew on. Jesus had been crucified six hours earlier. At the Temple the ceremonies to prepare Passover were underway. Soon blood would flow from butchered lambs. At Golgotha it was the end. Jesus expired. Those Jews best disposed to him cried their distress at what they saw as additional proof, if proof were needed, that he was not God.

But the Evangelists balanced this with a subtler analysis. According to one version, the centurion overseeing the

*When they had finished crucifying him
they shared out his clothing by casting
lots, and then sat down and stayed
there keeping guard over him*

(Matt. 27, 35–36).

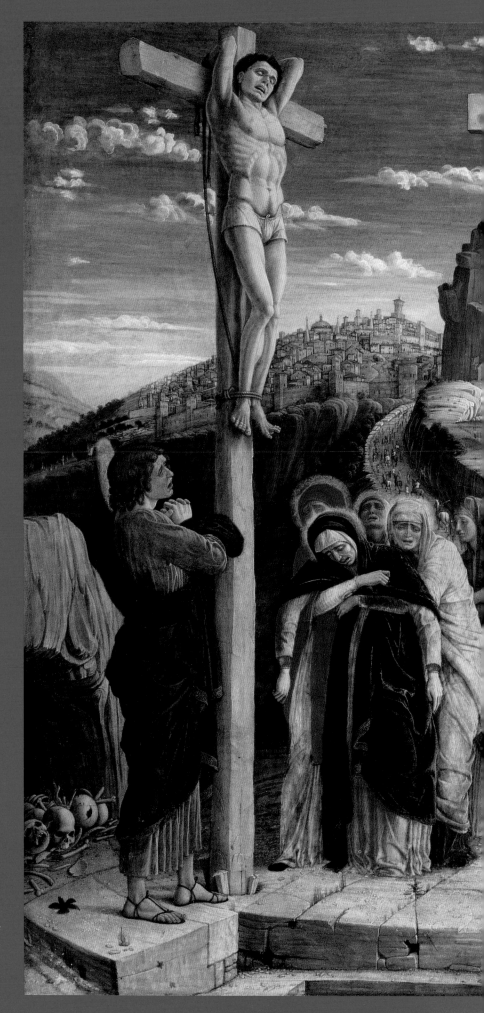

It was the third hour when they crucified him. The inscription giving the charge against him read "The King of the Jews"
(Mark 15:25–26).

Then they took the body of Jesus and bound it with linen cloths with the spices following the Jewish burial custom. At the place where he had been crucified there was a garden and in this garden a new tomb in which no one had been buried (John 19:40–41).

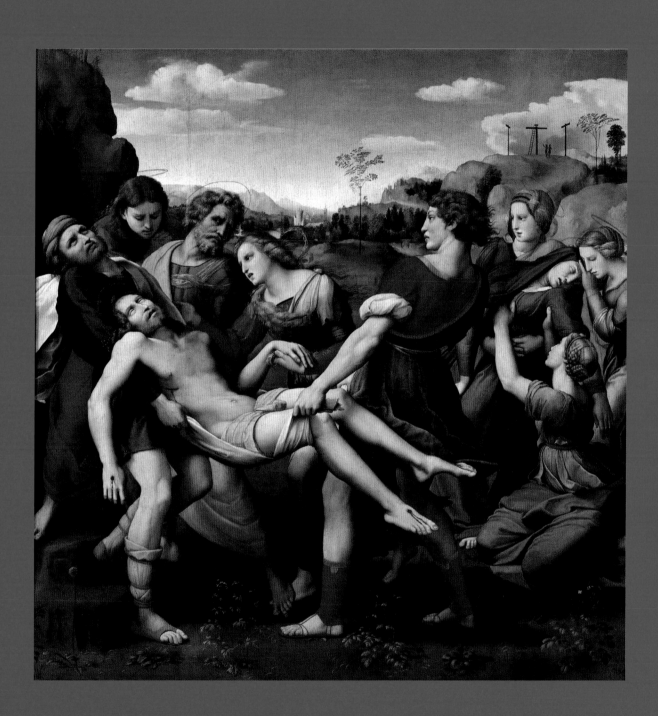

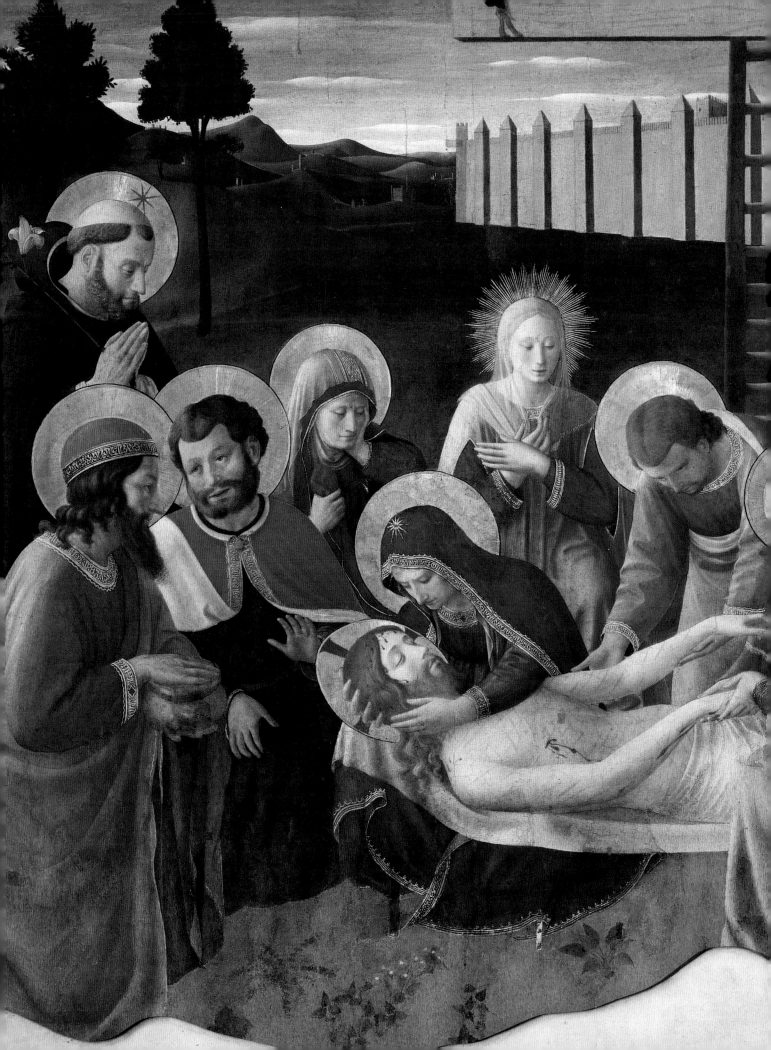

*He then took it down, wrapped it in a shroud and put it in the tomb which was hewn in stone
and which had never held a body. It was Preparation Day and the Sabbath was beginning to grow light*

(Luke 23:53–54).

ANDREA MANTEGNA. *THE LAMENTATION OVER THE DEAD CHRIST.*
1480—84. PINACOTECA DI BRERA. MILAN.

execution exclaimed: "Truly this man was the Son of God."
While another has it that he said: "Truly, this was a righteous
man." This should not it seems be interpreted as betraying
sudden conversion: in a Mediterranean world influenced by
Greek culture, the expression "Son of God" was a familiar
way of designating a great man. Jesus died and, according to
Mark, the veil of the Temple was torn asunder. Though this
surely did not actually occur (moreover, there was more than
one veil), by it Mark meant that henceforth the center of faith
was not at the Temple but in Christ. The apostles and the first
Christians continued for some time to attend the Temple.
Furthermore Matthew added that the earth trembled and
that the "tombs opened and the bodies of many holy people
rose from the dead" (Matt. 27:52). This is a reference to
texts in Holy Writ that announced the advent of the new
world inaugurated by the Resurrection.

Jesus died. According to John, the legionaries broke the
legs of the two other victims so as to hasten their demise. This
was not necessary for Jesus, and John makes clear: "Because all
this happened to fulfill the words of scripture: Not one bone
of his will be broken" (John 19:36). In the same way, Jesus
was lanced in his side—pointlessly since he was already dead.
But there again the Scripture corroborated a phrase from the
prophet Zechariah. "They will look to the one whom they
have pierced" (John 19:36).

Then a notable Jew, Joseph of Arimathea, wealthy enough
to possess a garden and a tomb (a rare thing) at the gate of
Jerusalem came forth. He had been close to Jesus. He would
ask Pilate to have the body removed to prevent its being
thrown into a communal grave with other felons. It would
have to be done quickly since the Passover feast was about to
begin. Nicodemus, another important person, pleaded with
Joseph and Pilate let them have their way. Rapidly, the two
men embalmed the body and wrapped it in a shroud. The
entombment was attended only by some women: no text
mentions Mary expressly, though she would often be pictured
with the body of her son on her lap.

Speed was of the essence. According to Matthew, emissaries from the high priests asked Pilate to set guards near
the tomb to prevent Jesus' disciples from snatching the body
to make it seem as though he had come back to life. And
Pilate granted their wish too. But this account comprises
such improbabilities that it is rejected as unhistorical by
every exegete.

For Matthew, whose text came much later than the other
Gospels, what mattered was to show that the apostles could
not possibly have emptied the tomb two days later. He thus
hoped to refute objections regarding the announcement of an
event so many people find unbelievable: the Resurrection.

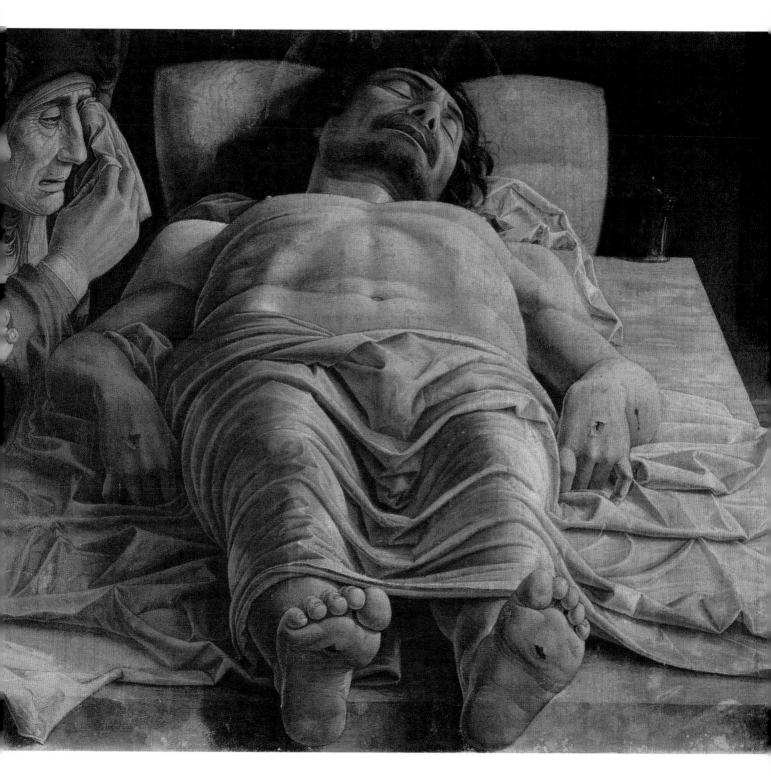

The Cross

The Greek word stauros employed in the Gospels to designate the Cross means only "pile," "post," or "upright" to which hanged, impaled, or crucified men might be attached (in the latter case a crossbeam would be inserted into a notch on the post). To this the condemned man was bound or nailed. Death was slow since no vital function was affected, though Jesus would have succumbed more speedily due to the dreadful torture he suffered in the night. The cross was a most shameful torment, reserved for slaves, foreigners and the "lower orders," as the Romans put it. It was as widely practiced by the Greeks as the Romans: the governor of Syria is said to have crucified twenty thousand Jews in 4 BCE. Contrary to what is often affirmed, the Jews also made use of it, as Flavius Josephus makes clear.

Jesus would have carried the crossbeam all the way to Golgotha. Forked poles would have been used to hoist the cross upright with him attached to it. On certain beams a narrow seat or footrest would be nailed. Not out of mercy, but on the contrary, to prolong and intensify the suffering: the victim would be tempted to let his weight fall on it so as to straighten up and gulp some air into his lungs—but once the effort proved too much, he would slump back exhausted and his flesh would be torn more horrifically still.

Christians adopted the cross as a symbol relatively early, even though the divinity of Jesus is better embodied in the Resurrection, an event more difficult to depict. The gesture of the "sign of the cross" was introduced by the Greek Saint Basil in the fourth century. Early Christians regarded the cross as a sign of glory. In the Apocalypse of Peter, an apocryphal Gospel widely read and commented upon by the Christians of the East from the second to fourth centuries, the cross was pictured as advancing before Jesus "upon clouds of heaven." In yet another text, the Gospel of Peter, it left the tomb at the same time as Jesus and spoke. A poet and bishop of Poitiers in the sixth century, Venantius Fortunatus, hailed the cross in these words: "Most glorious tree, dazzling, and adorned in royal purple."

Subsequently, stress fell above all on the pain and torment of Golgotha, before reverting to a symbol of glory: the sign of victory of the Son of Man, of God become Man.

ANDREA MANTEGNA, *ST. ZENO ALTARPIECE: THE CRUCIFIXION*, 1457–59. LOUVRE, PARIS.

Judas

Judas Iscariot was an individual whose enigmatic personality and reasons for betraying Jesus have aroused a vast array of questions and hypotheses. The nickname "Iscariot" means that it is likely he came from Kerioth, a small town in Judea, which would apparently make him the only apostle to originate in that part of Palestine, all the others being Galileans.

The Gospels indicate that his father was called Simon and that he acted as "treasurer" to the little community around Jesus. John the Evangelist, the most severe, adds that he was not averse to treating the fund as his own since he was a "thief." Could it have been the lure of money that spurred him to betray Jesus to the high priests? They did after all pay him thirty silver pieces (sicles or shekels, and not thirty deniers, as certain translations have it) for his treason. This was no negligible sum: it would, for example, have purchased a slave. But, at no more than four months wages for a farm laborer, it was no fortune either. Such a reward could never have motivated Judas to deliver up someone of Jesus' status. In fact, it would appear that the Evangelists quote this figure in reference to a biblical text ascribed to the prophet Zechariah that features many allusions to the Messiah awaited by the Jews. In it can be found a story concerning certain "sheep-dealers" who had designs on a herd and paid thirty shekels of silver to a shepherd, to whom the Lord exclaimed: "Throw it to the smelter, this princely sum at which they have valued me" (Zech. 11:13).

That Judas did the deed for money is thus doubtful. Others have suggested that Judas acted out of jealousy because he bore Jesus an exclusive love, a passion that verged on hatred. One further explanation may be advanced: his gesture was aimed at pushing Jesus into performing a spectacular act—all that the disciples expected of him, a kind of coup d'état.

There is also a more basic explanation: evil lurks in the heart of every man. Jesus, who knew it, instead of cursing him, felt sorry for him.

Pilate

Pilate belonged to the Roman gentry. Before being named procurator and prefect of Judea in the year 26 (the procurator was in charge of the administration—readily delegated to the chief priests—while the prefect held sway over the police and the soldiery), he had followed a military career.

Presented as vacillating in accounts of the Passion in the Gospels, Pilate in fact boasted a reputation for intransigence and contempt for the Jews that is seemingly justified by several incidents. He had minted coins bearing Roman cultic symbols, considered pagan in the eyes of the Jews. Furthermore in building an aqueduct to Jerusalem—where water consumption could soar at pilgrimage time—he had dipped into the sacred treasury of the Temple, thereby igniting an uprising that he repressed fearfully. Contrary to a regulation, which the occupying forces had themselves issued, by night he had also had brought into the city standards emblazoned with the effigy of the emperors the Romans treated as divinities. In protest to this the Jews marched to Caesarea, Pilate's usual residence. Lastly, the Gospel of Luke refers to the death of pilgrims from Galilee "whose blood Pilate had mingled with that of their sacrifices" (Luke 3:1). The sacrifices were animals, but the exact circumstances in which these pilgrims were killed is unknown.

One point is certain: Pilate was on excellent terms with the high priest Caiaphas. The latter remained in power for eighteen years—if often under the thumb of the family of his father-in-law Annas—an exceptional feat. Pilate was prefect of Judea for only ten years, from 26 to 36. He lost his post on orders from the emperor following a petition from the Samaritans concerning the mistreatment meted out to them by his men. Occupied countries enjoyed the right to appeal to Rome against the prefect, as can be deduced from Pilate's hesitation regarding the fate of Jesus when Christ's adversaries threatened to call him to account with Caesar. Pilate dragged down Caiaphas in his fall. Historians are of the opinion that this was no coincidence.

THE RESURRECTION

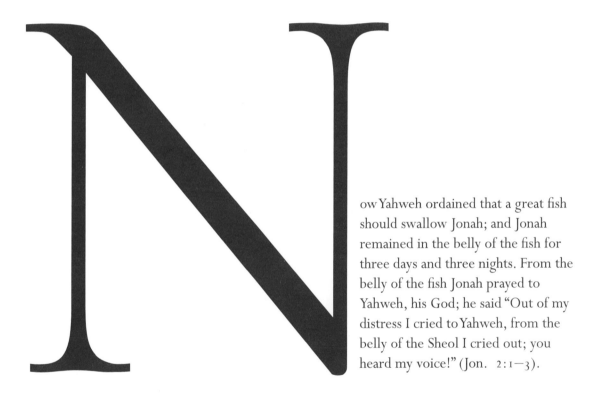

ow Yahweh ordained that a great fish should swallow Jonah; and Jonah remained in the belly of the fish for three days and three nights. From the belly of the fish Jonah prayed to Yahweh, his God; he said "Out of my distress I cried to Yahweh, from the belly of the Sheol I cried out; you heard my voice!" (Jon. 2:1–3).

He said to her,"Woman, why are you weeping? Who are you looking for?" Supposing him to be the gardener, she said, "Sir, if you have taken him away, tell me where you have put him, and I will go and remove him"

(John 20:15).

THE THIRD DAY

Dawn broke. Mary Magdalene could bear it no longer. During the Sabbath, she had been forbidden to go anywhere. What she was doing all these hours, what she was thinking, what beliefs she might have entertained, none can say. She too most probably concluded that once again death had had the last word.

That morning, as the sun peeked over the mountains to the east dappling Jerusalem in pink, she ran off to Jesus' tomb. It was not her hope to bear witness to some incredible event: simply, together with the other women who followed the path of Jesus as he journeyed to his death, she had prepared perfumes and aromatics, perhaps because she thought that Joseph of Arimathea and Nicodemus, being men, might have hurried the embalming of the corpse—or perhaps it was due to the Jewish custom of visiting the dead on the third day—that is, two days after the interment—to bring them aromatics.

She had abandoned all hope. The others that followed her, faithful women whose names the Evangelists do not even bother to record, could cherish no hopes either. And here they found the stone rolled back and figures clad in white, who told them that the Jesus whose body they sought was not to be found there, for the simple, unaccountable reason that he was alive.

Yes, alive. In the Gospel of John, the messengers did not even have time to tell Mary Magdalene that Jesus was risen. Hardly had she said, "they have taken my Lord away and I do not know where they have put him" (John 20:13)—she had no inkling that he could have risen, thinking rather of some trick on the part of the high priests' clan—hardly had the thought occurred to her that, even dead, even reduced to the state of a corpse, Jesus still disturbed the powerful, than she looked behind. She perceived an individual, whom she first took for a gardener. She at first even suspected him of having helped to purloin the body. But finally he allowed her to see him. It was he, Jesus, though she didn't recognize him immediately. The apostles, too, would find it hard to identify him. For he was the same, yet other; he had passed into another life. Both here and elsewhere.

"Why do you look among the dead for someone who is alive? He is not here: he has risen"

(Luke 24:5).

He charged her with a mission. He charged all the women with a mission. This was an extraordinary privilege that many Fathers of the Church would skirt around and whose underlying reasons they do not bother to elucidate. This exceptional merit was a response to their keeping the faith. Since it was they who hurried to the tomb as soon as they were able.

Mary Magdalene ran off, overjoyed, fulfilled, relieved. When the women told the apostles the news, according to Luke: "This story of theirs seemed pure nonsense and they did not believe them" (Luke 24:11). They thought it was nonsense, old wives' tales. The disciples at Emmaus, moreover, did not believe it for a second either, and although they listened, although they knew the tomb was empty, they wandered off, in despair. It was an attitude that earned them a rebuke from Jesus when they met him: "You foolish men! So slow to believe all that the prophets have said!" (Luke 24:25). "Slow" is a precise and pregnant word. There exist then realities that the heart can understand quicker and better than leaden reason.

Still, Peter did go to look in the tomb, in the company of another whose name is not given. They could see just the binding strips and shroud in which the corpse was enveloped. Peter, as Luke puts it, went away "amazed at what had happened" (Luke 24:12). John says: "Till this moment they had still not understood the Scripture that he must rise from the dead. The disciples then went back home" (John 20:9—10). They might have been slow to understand; but how could anyone believe in the incredible? Jesus, it is true, did not rise out of the tomb in a blaze of glory. The humility of God reached that far. He died in front of the people—but rose again without witnesses—contrary to what one sees in so many masterpieces and less elaborate depictions. A spectacular emergence from the tomb would have smacked of divine vengeance and the belittling of man. Leaving the sepulcher in front of sworn witnesses acknowledged by historians would have amounted to an attack on the freedom of mankind. If God were so obvious, people would be simply be machines made for worshiping him. On the evening of the Last Supper, Philip, one of the Twelve, had asked Jesus: "Lord, show us the Father and then we shall be satisfied" (John 14:8).

And Jesus told him to look at him instead, the master, the companion with whom they crisscrossed the country, who had been hungry and thirsty like them, who had suffered like them, who unsure of what lay in store for him, and for whom they were so afraid.

He was saying then that he was God. Difficult to credit, today still. But this very difficulty is the price of the freedom. And without freedom there can be no true love.

So the Resurrection was not an obvious marvel, like the rising sun. But to help people believe in it, to steady the faith, Jesus later gave them signs: appearances.

Now while he was with them at table, he took the bread and said the blessing; then he broke it and handed it to them. And their eyes were opened and they recognized him

(Luke 24:30–31).

THE APPEARANCES

·:·················:·

In the year 55, a good score of years therefore after the event, Paul drew up a list of these manifestations in his First Epistle to the Corinthians: Jesus "appeared to Cephas; and later to the twelve; and he appeared to more than five hundred of the brothers at the same time, most of whom are still with us, though some have fallen asleep; then, he appeared to James, and then to all the apostles. Last of all he appeared to me, as though I was a child born abnormally" (1 Cor. 15:5–8).

The James of whom he speaks is the one he calls "the brother of the Lord" and whom he had met in Jerusalem the first time he went there having heard Jesus on the way to Damascus. Cephas is patently Peter. Paul's list is incomplete. First of all, the women, mentioned by Matthew, Mark, and John, are omitted. As are the two disciples at Emmaus. And lastly John recounts (21:1–23) that Jesus also appeared on the banks of the Lake of Tiberias to a group around Peter, composed of Thomas, Nathanael, two sons of Zebedee, and two other unnamed disciples. Subsequently in his account John refers to the "disciple whom Jesus loved" as a witness to the scene, but he remains anonymous. It is with them, after a miraculous draft of fishes, that Jesus shared the bread and part of the catch. Together, they ate.

Life had reverted to routine. If they were still busy fishing (John says they had already seen Jesus before on two occasions), then life was going on as normal. They still had to eat. Just as following the miracle of the loaves and fishes, its beneficiaries still had to make or buy bread for themselves. Life went on. These astonishing, amazing events had not taken place in some parallel universe. People still had to earn a living, to eat, to sleep.

Jesus remained the same. But utterly changed. Not a ghost: a ghost does not consume grilled fish, a ghost does not have its wounds fingered by that incredulous apostle, Thomas Didymus. No immaterial specter: the Gospel of John, twice describes how Jesus appeared to the disciples while they were in hiding.

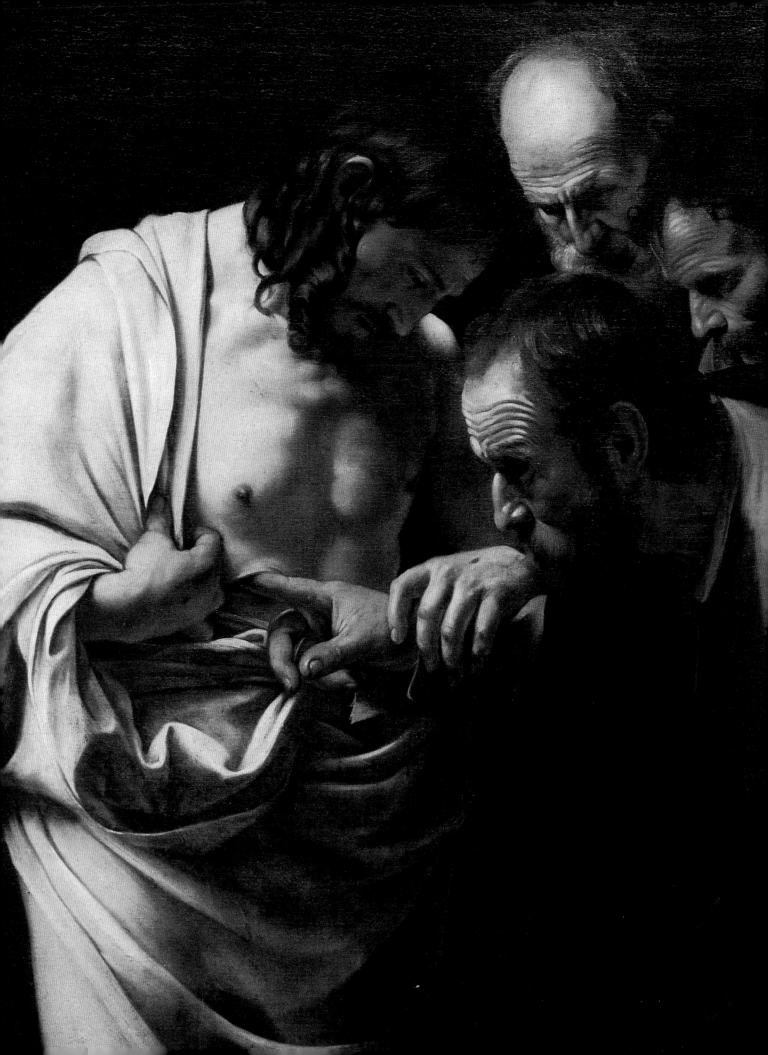

"Unless I can see the holes that the nails made
in his hands and can put my finger into
the holes they made and unless I can put my hand
into his side, I refuse to believe"

(John 20:25).

After this, he showed himself under another form to two of them as they were on their way to the country. These went back and told the others, who did not believe them either

(Mark 16:12–13).

For Jesus was of course everywhere.

Neither was he a risen corpse, like one might imagine Lazarus to be, for example. Jesus' body was transfigured. It had become a spiritual body. This is the expression Paul employs in the First Epistle to Corinthians (15:44): a *soma pneumatikon*, in Greek. It is certainly difficult, or rather impossible, to imagine such a thing. A spiritual body is not even gaseous. It is both a real body and totally spiritual.

The chief implication is that it no longer experiences the limits intrinsic to the human body, through which one can act and communicate, but which also prevents acting and communicating as well perfectly. The body of the resurrected Christ was a body with boundless potential; not a body denied, as it is often believed. It was exempt from the normal conditions of earthly life, but it could also be subject to them. It was liberated. Yet visible. In the Gospels, the Greek word *opte* reoccurs several times, from the verb *orao,* meaning: "he showed himself," "he let himself be seen." The apostles and the others did not dream. You don't risk your life because you meet someone in a dream.

And risk their lives they did.

They certainly did not remove the body to spread the rumor of a resurrection: neither the high priests nor the Romans—who would have surely wanted to have exposed such an act—seem to have bothered to enquiry into it in any way.

And if the disciples had hidden the body, would they all have kept quiet, and endured martyrdom and torture?

Finally, and the point bears repetition, they were first told of the Resurrection by women. If the disciples had carried off the body in a desperate attempt to deceive the populace into thinking the crucified Jesus was still alive, the surest means of discrediting the whole idea would be to have the Resurrection proclaimed by women, whoever they might be.

There can be no proof of the Resurrection. Only witnesses, who moreover made no attempt whatsoever to see or hear Jesus again: it was always Jesus who took the initiative "to let himself be seen." These men, fleeing, hiding, in despair, dreaming only of getting back to Galilee, then rallied and were prepared to confront all-comers in their desire to proclaim that Jesus was alive—and the best proof was that they had seen him, that they had even supped with him.

Some event certainly took place then, something like an explosion, a sudden upwelling of faith that changed, that overwhelmed them. And they stated that this event was their meeting with a living, resurrected Jesus, and this they repeated until they died on its account.

TINTORETTO. *THE ASCENSION*. 1578–81.
REDENTORE, VENICE.

THE ASCENSION

·:· ················· ·:·

Christ's Ascension, marking the end of his terrestrial presence, and therefore of his visibility, has interested artists more than the Evangelists, and the theologians and exegetes who followed in their wake. The Gospels of Matthew and John do not even mention it. Mark's text, having reported appearances by Jesus on the day of Passover, states baldly: "And so the Lord Jesus, after he had spoken to them, was taken up into heaven; there at the right hand of God he took his place" (Mark 16:19). Luke is not much more forthcoming. He briefly relates that after giving instructions to his disciples, Jesus "then took them out as far as Bethany, and raising his hands, he blessed them. Now as he blessed them, he withdrew from them and was carried up to heaven" (Luke 24:50–51). The Acts of the Apostles by the same Luke is the only text to provide a thorough account: it is through the Holy Spirit that Jesus was carried off, not on the evening of Passover but forty days later. At that time, as the apostles gazed up at the sky, two angels told them that their wait would be fruitless: "This Jesus who has been taken up from you into heaven will come back in the same way as you have seen him go into heaven" (Acts 1:11).

Of course, such texts need decoding. If Luke in the Acts of the Apostles places the Ascension forty days after Passover, it is because of the idea of plenitude conveyed by the figure forty: David and Solomon each reigned for forty years; Moses remained on Mount Sinai forty days and forty nights; after his baptism, Jesus stayed in the wilderness for forty days. And if the account in has it that when Jesus rose "a cloud took him from their sight" (Acts 1:9), it was a recollection of the cloud that came over the people of Israel on their return from Egypt under Moses' aegis (Ex. 40:36–38). In other words, it was the sign, in this event, of the presence of God.

The sense of the word "heaven" also calls for elucidation. Even if the Apostles' Creed declares that Jesus "descended" then "ascended into heaven," those reciting it no longer think of the space through which the planet revolves.

The distinction between heaven and earth symbolizes the distinction between God and Man; above mankind, the role of heaven, or the sky, is to express the transcendence of God. Moreover, according to the Gospel of John, Jesus himself spoke another language. At the Last Supper he repeated seven times: "I am in the Father." And when he appeared to Mary Magdalene on the morning of Passover he told her: "Do not cling to me [or, in other translations, "touch me not"] because I have not ascended to the Father. But go to the brothers, and tell them: I am ascending to my Father and your Father, to my God and your God" (John 20:17).

Furthermore, the Ascension concerned all the "brethren," since Jesus said "your Father." It stands then for the progress of humanity as a whole to God, who is not to be found in any geographical or spatial location. Although Saint Augustine, who lived at the turn of the third and fourth centuries, wrote that the feast of the Ascension had been instituted by the apostles themselves, it was only in his own time that it became widespread. It was then sometimes celebrated at the same time as Pentecost, that is, fifty days after Easter: it was thought (and certain Churches keep to this) that Jesus, following his departure, had not tarried before sending the Holy Spirit. In any case it is believed that God is ever present at the side of the Man. When Mark wrote that Jesus sat "at the right hand of God" (Mark 16:19), he meant that he was glorified. And through Jesus, being God-Man, it was humanity, which was exalted in him, since Jesus did not play the role of a man for a few years and then divest himself of humanity. It still resides within him.

POSTQVA VENERVT IN LOCVM QVI DICITVR CALVARIE CRVCIFIXERVT EV.LV.XXIII.

SCEDIT SVP CELOS ZVOLAVIT SVP PEÑAS VENTORVM·PS·XVII·C~

HS YHVS POSTO LOCVTVS E ASSVTVS E ICELVM. M. VLTIMO.

IDI DNM SEDEEM SVPER SOLIV EXCELSV 7 ELEVATVM 7 PLENA DOM MAIESTAE EI. YSA.VI

When Pentecost day came round, they had all met together when suddenly there came from heaven
a sound as of a violent wind that filled the entire house in which they were sitting

(Acts 2:1–2).

PENTECOST

•:⋯⋯⋯⋯⋯:•

On the occasion of the pilgrimage festival during which pious Jews would go up to the Temple, Jesus' family and companions too returned to Jerusalem to pray together. At Qumran, it was even the "supreme feast day." Its purpose was to commemorate the arrival of Moses and his people in the Sinai. According to Exodus (12:1–3), God instructed them to leave Egypt on the tenth of the first month of the year; according to the same book (Ex. 19:1), they had arrived in the Sinai a month and half later. Hence Jews thus celebrated the feast on the forty-ninth day (*he pentekoste*, in Greek) following Passover. It was also a feast of the "first fruits," a harvest festival and a day of thanksgiving during which, after the seven weeks that on average the harvest lasted, the first fruits of the earth were offered to God, the source of all good.

They assembled there and then, according to Luke (Acts 2:1–8), to pray. To replace Judas, they had chosen and then drawn by lot between two "candidates" a certain Matthias (of which nothing is known). And so they prayed. Then there came a violent gust of wind, and the text describes "tongues of fire" spouting above them. And at once they began to speak in various different languages. The Spirit Jesus foresaw had come upon them. Perhaps they weren't expecting it on that day. Jesus had said to the Pharisee Nicodemus shortly before his death: "The wind blows where it pleases; you can hear its sound, but you cannot tell where it comes from or where it is going" (John 3:8). The tongues of fire described by Luke, the chief author of the Acts of the Apostles, are perhaps a symbolic reference to remarks by Jesus he reports in his Gospel: "I have come to bring fire to the earth, and how I wish it were blazing already" (Luke 12:49). The phenomenon also recalls the many references to fire in the Bible: through it, the presence and the glory of God were made manifest in, among other things, the burning bush in which God appeared to Moses; the column of fire that led the Hebrews in the Exodus; and in the brightness of the sky at the Nativity. For early Christians, the light and heat of fire were akin to the

GIOTTO. *PENTECOST.*
C. 1303–05. CAPPELLA
DEI SCROVEGNI. PADUA.

radiation of the divine Spirit: it purified those it approached, illuminating and warming them. And if the fire was divided into "tongues," perhaps this is a reference to foreign languages: the Greek word is the same. Readers of Luke understood the significance of these expressions, which allowed them, better than it does us today, to grasp a deeper meaning. If the author tells us that at once the apostles—men who would have known only Aramaic, a smattering of Hebrew, and perhaps a few words of Greek—began to "speak in tongues," it means that they were henceforth able to announce the good news of God to all the nations, instead of hurrying off to Galilee or locking themselves up in the "upper room" in Jerusalem to pray.

Jesus, each time he appeared, gave them fresh impetus for their mission. This time the Holy Spirit repeated the injunction, urging them to go abroad; Peter obeyed and sallied forth into Jerusalem. More still, the Holy Spirit enjoined them to leave, much against their will, the very frontiers of Israel, to go beyond the boundaries of the Law. For, as future events would demonstrate, in fact Pentecost occurred in successive phases, forming a sort of chain in the Acts of the Apostles. First of all,

Samaria was evangelized by Philip, and the Samaritans "received the Holy Spirit" (Acts 8:17) from the hands of Peter and John. Focusing initially on the heathen, Paul's choice of mission was similarly ordained by the Holy Spirit (Acts 13:2), who also directed the same Paul to venture to Europe (Acts 16:6–10).

The most significant episode in this respect occured with the meeting between Peter and the centurion Cornelius (Acts 10). Commanding a contingent named the "Italian band" stationed in Cesarea, the procurator's capital, this Roman officer was a pious man. One day he had a vision. An "Angel of the Lord" ordered him to start a search for Peter, who lodged not far off, in a village called Joppa, with a "tanner." Cornelius did as he was bidden. His emissaries found Peter in a puzzled state, pondering a vision of his own—concerning the "clean" and "unclean"—whose meaning was not obvious to him. Nevertheless, he agreed to follow them back in the company of a few Christians from Joppa, Jews like him. So Paul met the centurion surrounded by friends and relations. Paul held back, unsure what he was doing in such a place: for it was forbidden for a Jew to mix with "people of another race and visit them"

(Acts 10:28). Perhaps he was going too far. Then, all of a sudden, he understood his dream: "God has no favorites, but anybody of any nationality who fears him and does what is right is acceptable to him" (Acts 10:34–35). Paul then told this little group of heathens about what Jesus did in Israel, about his Resurrection and the mission he entrusted to "certain witnesses that God had chosen beforehand" (Acts: 10:41).

At this point, Peter—who had not yet grasped the full import of events—added that this mission was addressed to the "People," that is, to Jews alone. Then the Holy Ghost, halting Peter in his tracks, intervened and "fell" on all his listeners. All the Christians of Jewish origin accompanying the apostle were "astonished" to see that the gift of the Holy Spirit appeared among the pagans too, who, in their turn, promptly started speaking in tongues. Then Peter baptized them. To overcome Peter's reticence and misgivings, God had been forced to drive the point home: an unforeseeable choice, that of a senior officer of the Roman occupation; two visions; delegations; and then the spectacular intervention of the Spirit itself, sent this time to the non-Jewish and not to those who prayed to the Holy spirit in Jerusalem. So the baptismal rite performed by Peter simply ratified a decision already ordained by God.

The Holy Spirit was to struggle still to be heard. For back in Jerusalem Peter had to confront the Jewish Christians: what, they accused, had he rubbed shoulders with the uncircumcised and broken bread with them? The outrage! He had to tell them the whole story. Adding, "and who was I to stand in God's way?" (Acts: 11:17). Only then did they finally calm down, still surprised that God had given the same grace to pagans. Were they then forced to share their God, the God of Jesus? Having learned that in Antioch, in Syria, emigrant Jews were also preaching the good news, the people of Jerusalem dispatched one of them, Barnabas, a member of the lower clergy of the Temple. And it was in Antioch, according to the Acts of the Apostles, that, for the first time, the disciples took on the name of Christians.

The sequence of Pentecosts had finally put an end to all their hesitations, indecisions, and exclusions. Jesus had been heard. Christianity had been born for all peoples.

The Disciples At Emmaus

Two men were walking towards Emmaus a few kilometers from Jerusalem—it's unsure exactly where, towards the unknown, a place of lost hopes. Both men were drained of hope, of enthusiasm. They had believed that Jesus would deliver the world from evil, Israel from the aristocracy of the Temple and from the Roman occupiers. They might well have been assistants to the apostles, men who would invite the deserving to come and listen to Jesus, occasionally planning his trips, keeping the mob away when it came too close, or else comforting those unable to get near enough. They too had sacrificed everything. And now it was all over. Jesus had died without lifting a finger to defend himself, abandoned even by his closest companions. And all they could do was to chew over their regrets, their resentment, their remorse.

At least they could talk about it between themselves, sharing their feelings of bitterness. They were not totally withdrawn and that's already quite a lot. Open-minded, they meditated and conversed. So open were they that when a stranger joined them, they told him all about their misfortune and their suffering. They knew nothing of him, but they were amazed that he was so little aware of what was going on back in Jerusalem, so unheeding of things that touched them to the quick. So they explained it all and told him that the body of Jesus had vanished—an event that had exacerbated their despair. Maybe then they had got it all wrong. The unknown man took them up on this, but he did not yet reveal who he was.

Then, as the Gospel of Luke puts it, the man explained to them the history of the world starting from Moses and the prophets. Their hearts, warming, opened up still more: then they burned. Still they failed to recognize him, since resurrected he appeared otherwise, but the Scriptures, such as he expounded them, made it plain enough. So they took a meal together. Jesus had always insisted that eating was a time for sharing, and had spoken of a meal from which no one would ever be excluded. Not even those who recognized him too late. For it was never too late. And so they set out once again for Jerusalem.

PETER PAUL RUBENS, *CHRIST AT EMMAUS*, C. 1630.
MUSEO DEL PRADO, MADRID.

Thomas Didymus

Thomas was not present, so John (20:19–29) tells us, when the resurrected Jesus appeared to the assembled apostles for the first time shortly after the Sabbath. He did not believe them when they told him of a scene that was incredible for so many. Again according to John, Jesus returned a week later and asked Thomas to touch the wounds he still had in his hands and side.

Finally convinced, Thomas exclaimed: "My Lord and my God!" And Jesus replied: "You believe because you can see me. Blessed are those who have not seen and yet believe" (John 20:29). This sentence was addressed to humanity down the generations. Because of this scene, the apostle is often dubbed "doubting" Thomas. But in the Gospel of John, the only one to refer to him (the other three Evangelists quoted the name only once in the list of the twelve), he is also called "Didymus," which means "the twin." Whose twin? No clues are given.

Thomas is mentioned three times by John. First, in the narrative of the resurrection of Lazarus. When Jesus decided to go to Bethany, even though the risk was great in a locality so close to Jerusalem, it was enigmatic Thomas who remarked, perhaps courageously, perhaps ironically: "Let us also go to die with him" (John 11:16). Then, at the Last Supper, when Jesus told the disciples that they knew the path he was about to follow, Thomas protested: "Lord, we do not know where you are going, so how can we know the way?" (John 14:5) to which Jesus replied: "I am the Way; I am the Truth and Life" (John 14:6).

And finally, after the Resurrection, having touched Jesus' wounds, Thomas exclaimed: "My Lord and my God!" (John 20:28)—one of the most powerful assertions of the divinity of Jesus to be found in the Gospels.

Thomas thus seems to have played the role of the doubter so that Jesus could make manifest his essence—and so that he could be acknowledged by the incredulous.

Paul

Paul, a Jew born at Tarsus (in present-day Turkey), was a Roman citizen, who, before leaving for Jerusalem, had undertaken lengthy studies. He was a strict Pharisee who insisted on the meticulous observance of the Law. So he took part in the persecution of the first Christians, "breathing threats to slaughter the Lord's disciples," (Acts 9:1). Thus stirred to violence, he went off to find the high priest and ask him for letters of introduction to the synagogues of Damascus, a city with some Christians he wanted to bring back to Jerusalem in chains. On the way there, he was engulfed in a light that left him blinded and the resurrected Jesus spoke to him. He promptly converted.

The account of Paul's conversion in Acts and the less demonstrative one in his own Epistle to Galatians (Gal. 1:13–16)—emigrants from Gaul who had settled in the third century BCE in Cappadocia—concord on one point: this conversion, this total reversal, did not spring from reflection, from a dialog with some Christian, but was the work of Jesus himself showing the apostle that he lived.

The Epistle Paul wrote to the Corinthians in summer 51 (the date is certain) was the first written record of the Resurrection. Thereafter, following heated debates with "Peter and James, the brother of Jesus," as he called him himself, Paul became apostle to the pagans among whom he proselytized on three crucial missionary journeys. Arrested in Jerusalem and imprisoned for two years in Cesarea, he was then transferred to Rome and died there.

Paul's influence on Christian doctrine was considerable. At the heart of his faith stood the Cross: the death of Jesus was, he underlined, the work of scrupulous observers of the Jewish Law, not of impious souls. It thus should be concluded that while "the Law is holy" (Rom. 7:12), it could be perverted by sin. For Paul, sin was an evil that pervaded humankind. You could not escape it by just wanting to be pure, or through the strict observance of the Law, of any law, but only by accepting the unconditional love of God.

And I saw the dead, great and small alike, standing in front of his throne while the books lay open. And another book was opened, which is the book of life, and the dead were judged from what was written in the books, as their deeds deserved

(Apoc. 20:12).

MICHELANGELO,
THE LAST JUDGMENT, 1536—41.
SISTINE CHAPEL, VATICAN.

Translated from the French by David Radzinowicz
Design: Atelier Juliane Cordes, Corinne Dury
Proofreading: Philippa Hurd
Typesetting: Thomas Gravemaker
Map: Thierry Renard
Production: Corinne Trovarelli
Color Separation: Dupont Photogravure, Paris

Biblical quotations are taken from
the New Jerusalem Bible.

Distributed in North America
by Rizzoli International Publications, Inc.

Simultaneously published in French as *Jésus*
© Flammarion, Paris, 2007

English-language edition
© Flammarion, 2007

www.editions.flammarion.com

07 08 09   3 2 1

ISBN-13: 978-2-0803-0017-1
Dépôt légal: 09/2007

Printed in Italy by Canale